Stay

Beyo

2020 Apertures

People are like stained-glass windows.
They sparkle and shine when the sun is out,
but when the darkness sets in,
their true beauty is revealed
only if there is light from within.

Elisabeth Kubler-Ross

Linda Varsell Smith

Acknowledgments

Window on Maureen Therrien Frank

Formatter and Illustrator
TheMandalaLady.com
My poetry friends, critique groups

intuitive consultants, family and friends.

Windows on

Copyright ©2020 By Rainbow Communications
ISBN: 978-1-716-24458-2
Rainbow Communications
471 NW Hemlock Ave.
Corvallis, Oregon 97330
varsell4@comcast.net

Window on Linda Varsell Smith

Poet trying to open windows and look beyond.

She is a teacher, poet and novelist from Corvallis, Oregon who lives with her husband Court in a miniature museum with collections of dollhouses, angels, Swedish Folk art, seasonal decorations. Linda retired from teaching creative writing, life story, children's literature and Literary Publication which produced the award-winning, The Eloquent Umbrella magazine for Linn-Benton Community College. She taught writing workshops, judges poetry contests for all ages. She gives readings and sponsors poetry events. She was an editor for Calyx Books for 32 years, is former president of the Oregon Poetry Association and is current president of PEN Women in Portland. Linda is a member of Marys Peak Poets, Poetic License, Children's Book Writers, Writing the Wrongs to Rights, part of the Women's March. She plays competitive and cooperative Scrabble and is a fan of dance, gymnastics, art, plays, physics and metaphysics.

Contents

How lucky I am to live in a home with windows. Against all odds– the encroachments of construction companies and lawn services and exterminators– these windows open onto a world that stubbornly insists on remaining wild.

Margaret Renkle

Spring in the Backgarth

Chi-Gathering in Spring

Spring Quarantine

Dandelion Dilemma

Chi-Gathering in Spring

Summer Quarantine

Remembering

Windows on the World

Window on the Cosmos

Spring in the Backgarth

Begin challenging your assumptions.
Your assumptions are the windows on the world.
Scrub them off every once in awhile
or the light won't come in.

Alan Alda

Spring in the Backgarth

Study color, texture, light,
shadow, life and death
with insight.

Explore patterns, cycles, sound
and temperature
in compound.

Witness changes, movements, signs
the garth is alive
with designs.

Spring blossoms and buds
as rain muds.

Garth

Our backyard ground hosts a garth,
orchard, garden, lawn.
soil of earth.

Lots of clay and added soil
for topsoil taken
with much toil.

The dirt has diverse covers
many plant, grassy
take-overs.

One-fifth acre home
to welcome.

Mower-Gardener

He tends, trims, plants in garden,
slaughters the lawn weeds.
No pardon.

Manicures lawn uniform,
diligent weeder
is his norm.

Organic steward hand-mows
and composts cast-offs.
Green–he knows.

Sees trees pruned, harvests,
passes tests.

Observer-Defender

She records and defends garth,
breathes deep, gathers chi,
loves weeds' worth.

Advocates diversity,
color, re-wilding.
Let garth be!

Dislikes mowing "weeds",
defends yellow spots
and their needs.

She writes poetry
as garth spy.

Chi Chair

In my black, metal, chi chair
I deep breath chi force
in fresh air.

I carry a soft blue pillow
to cushion the seat
to allow

meditation in comfort,
backyard reflections,
an effort

to loop earth to sky
mystery.

Walker

Tri-pod, walker Trinity
carries gear, pillow,
braces me.

Uneven stone and ground jar me.
I hold my grip tight,
sit down for some chi.

Blue frame folds, has cloth basket.
Does it like to haul?
Can't ask it.

Used to prevent falls,
my pitfalls.

Weather

Changeable, uncertain air
remains polluted
everywhere.

Whatever sky holds and drops,
transported by wind,
breaks and pops.

I sit and breathe in dry air.
I'm fair-weather friend.
I'm aware.

Weather creates mood—
prefer good.

Helicopter Weather Station

On top of shared fence with our
neighbor – white gizmo
wind-power?

Spins top like helicopter.
Wind whirls, but stays put.
I prefer

their artistic whirligig
like blooming lotus–
very big.

On neutral perch this
quiet hiss.

White Butterflies

I look for white butterflies,
they carry messages
space defies?

I think beloveds who passed
flitter by to check
on me—fast.

White butterflies comfort me
in my shut-in time,
lovingly.

My eyes follow flight,
with delight.

Birds

I'm bird watcher, not expert.
Can't name some of them.
Stay alert.

Stellar jays, sparrows, hummingbirds,
woodpeckers stop by.
I've lost words.

Artful antics entertain
with birdsongs and chirps—
bird refrain.

Graceful, so moving,
I'm loving.

Azaleas

Pink and red blooms spill over
bush to garden,
splotch cover.

Wildly sprawling limbs free-flow
no form boundaries
as suburbs grow.

Tight bloom clusters thrust their hues,
overpower the leaves,
few green clues.

Hide wooden fence.
Keep suspense.

Rhododendrons

Tall, bushy rhododendron.
Purple, pink, red to
gaze upon.

Birds hide in your lush limbs, rest
from their nit-picking
far from nest.

Rhodies is a short nickname.
Flowers not chickens
is their game.

Though they are flashy—
not trashy.

Chives

Purple chives or Allium thrive.
Can eat them I've heard
when called chive.

I'd rather look than eat them.
Not a salad fan.
Garden hem.

Gathered in one corner spot,
they guide garden hose
to the plot.

Lovely, purple bloom
makes some room.

Later-bloomers

Gladiolas and roses
await their blooms in
green poses.

After floral parade fades
they'll be center stage,
bright facades.

But now tucked away, unseen
unnoticed, they are
still in scene.

When they come in view.
praises due.

Dandelion Fan

I'm a dandelion groupie.
I'm dandelion strong.
I'm loopy?

Why am I such a support?
Mourn when they are mowed.
Make report?

They symbolize shine and strength.
They persevere, thrive
go great length.

They make me, hope, smile
for awhile.

Buttering Up Buttercups

As dandelions leave backyard,
buttercups arrive.
They try hard.

They glow yellow in clipped grass.
Some escape mower–
(metal ass).

Gentle petals splay for sun,
welcome bees' visits.
Status won.

Please help cheer me up
buttercup!

9

Weeds

Some slander flowers as weed.
I do not agree.
Weeds–indeed!

Dandelions and buttercups
are my favorite
pick me ups.

Yellow glowing orbs in grass
escape to garden,
safe alas.

Mowers chop off head.
Doom ahead.

Grass

Grass is a bland conformer,
same height and haircut.
I'm reformer.

Let flowers join boring blade,
lengthen mowing time,
growing aid.

Crabgrass invades makes tougher
tug, grass purity.
Life rougher.

These manicured lawns
bring on yawns.

Canopies

An orchard of apple, pear,
peach, plum, hazelnut–
all appear

to lace shadows across lawn.
Cherry tree chopped down.
Peach-no brawn.

Birds harvest edibles first.
We get some of them,
maybe worst.

Organic, not sprayed
are displayed.

Berry Patches

We've strawberry, blueberry
raspberry patches,
once cherry.

Their bushes flick white petals
awaiting the fruit,
like snow, falls.

Birds in bushes pick early.
Blueberries in fridge
picked dearly.

Berries enhance meal,
tasty deal.

Hose

Green, rubber, metal-nose hose,
slithers in garden,
as it goes.

Meanders like a scribble,
rolls up like a spring,
will dribble.

Moved for mower when in grass.
Lugged around, roughly,
tugged alas.

Long, slender, river—
life giver.

Watering Can

Watering can's proboscis
dribbles from its nose
like mucous.

Gray, metal, round, belly fat
with elephant snout—
dwell on that.

It waters plants and gets left,
knocked over, dismissed,
Is bereft?

It weathers each day
it will stay.

Feathers

Rarely feathers fall to ground.
I collect them. I
smile when found.

Most are blue from stellar jays,
some from small sparrow,
garner praise.

Intricate, delicate, light
they flare from a spine,
right for flight.

Angel good omen
from heaven.

Transient Creatures

Unseen or seen briefly they
explore the yard, come
night or day.

Squirrels, raccoons, dogs, rats and cats,
nutria, deer, birds,
maybe bats.

Bugs, bees, moths, winging kinds,
crawlers, opossums—
diverse finds.

Welcome to our garth,
outside hearth.

Pinwheel

Wind spins blue and white pinwheel
sky and cloud colors
dances reel.

It takes a gust for gusto
to create movement
make it go.

Resembles a flower yet
can not grow or fade,
just gets wet

Blooms on its stiff stalk,
tends to balk.

Wind Chimes

Dangling rods wind-clank for sound.
Wind dictates rhythm
when gust found.

Breezes too gentle to move
chimes to music,
so I love

the gusto of gusts. Strong winds
jingle, jangle tones
which reminds

me of the birdsongs
as rod bongs.

Airlika

Airlika, rusty angel
dangles from a branch,
holds up well.

Metal designs define her,
wears protective coat
from weather.

Her silent horn blows westward.
Wind sways her gently,
face forward.

She enchants my gaze
on all days.

Tootsie

Tootsie, angel weathervane,
toots her horn northwest,
gray as rain.

She does not move in the wind.
She seems stuck in place.
No whirlwind.

Does she not know her mission?
Does she wait for some
permission?

Steadfast, she holds own
earthly throne.

Bottom

He's a small concrete angel
sprawled on his back on
blue table.

Swath of cloth for privacy
across his loin with
accuracy.

A tennis ball at armpit
tiny toy version,
now not hit.

Coated to shine bright
to delight.

.

Blue Table

Small, round, blue, metal table
on the patio
is stable

place for glasses and Bottom
beside chi chair,
draw some om.

Bottom, cherubic angel
lazes and stares at
you as well.

Side table holds food.
All for good.

Metal Bluebird

Stuck on stalk between pavers
this bluebird can't fly—
no waivers.

This bluebird needs a good name.
Bluetiful will do,
but the same

fate to be inanimate.
But still conscious though?
Meditate?

Vacant— all surface?
Stays in place?

Patio

Narrow stone pavers make it.
No cover, mortar
that's just it.

A little wider than a chair.
Grass thrusts through the cracks,
in fresh air.

Uneven, so watch your step.
My walker gets stuck,
can misstep.

Re-directs the rain,
dries again.

Ladder

Tall ladder leans on house wall,
used to clear gutters,
catch-it-all.

Paint from its steps, shelf holds pail.
Clamber to roof top
check if fail.

Metal teepee frame without
tent cover, braces
all about.

It can stand on own,
when not prone.

Shed

Beige shed stores apples, hose,
hand tools, buckets and
things who knows?

Black roof like a cloud shadow,
stands beside office
back window.

Apples, newspaper-wrapped
put in boxes keep
'til unwrapped.

Like a quiet mouse,
edge of house.

Compost Pile

I do not often visit
this yard waste heap
deposit.

Small twigs, grass, leaves are the most
debris to breakdown
in compost.

Pruned branches, kitchen food waste
are in tall yard cart. Lid
closed with haste.

Pile our garden's wealth
makes mulch stealth.

Power Lines

Poles hold electric, cable,
electric wire feed,
disable

tall spruce limbs, whacked off its trunk—
Christmas tree top.
My heart sunk.

Bird rest stop like music notes
sing their birdsong, chill,
stay afloat.

Power lines scar sky,
our country.

Rock Wall

Chunks of sidewalk line in place.
Grass whiskers through cracks.
Beards surface.

Moss softens stone, gathers rain,
holds back upper tier
garden's plane.

Birds find a cushioned landing,
place to poke. Views
commanding.

Hard contrast to grass,
restrains mass.

Fences

Wooden fences on three sides
declare boundaries,
line decides.

Gaps in slats slices the view,
striped fauna, fauna
provide clue.

Some creatures through broken slats
slither between yards,
allow cats.

Fences can define
quarantine.

Facing the Backyard

Back of house has window wall,
for dry, warm, vista—
view of all.

The garth splays surface wonder,
unmarked burials
to ponder.

Slug slime, bird splat on siding,
spied looking south,
providing

blemishes on green
to be seen.

Fun in the Backyard

This Easter egg hunt canceled.
Money in plastic eggs
to stay sealed.

Balls thrown, water balloons leak.
Badminton, races,
hide and seek.

Golf course with tin cans for holes
mini-golf putts on lawn,
soccer goals.

Games, barbecues,
chase the blues.

Chi-Gathering in Spring

What you really want for yourself
is always trying to break through,
just as a cooling breeze flows through
an open window on a hot day.
Your part is to open the windows
of your mind.

Vernon Howard

Do I Stay or Do I Go?

Mid-afternoon I debate whether
to go into the backyard to chi-gather.
All day it rains then shines.

At the moment it is sunny. Sky
splits between gray in the west
and blue in the east.

Do I put on my shoes and walk
outside the wall of windows to my
wet chi chair? I could take my pillow.

As I try to decide, the crisp shadows
blur, fade, disappear as gray sky invades.
I am glad to stay inside.

The stellar jays and sparrows flit
among canopies more when it's
sunny. No white butterflies.

The lawn had one day after mowing
to recover. About four dandelions
and six buttercups are survivors.

The red rhododendrons look washed out,
lost their blush, bedraggled. Azaleas
a tad past their prime as well.

The pinwheel spins furiously
and clicks off any residual rain.
Wind chimes clang.

Tootsie, the angel weathervane,
seemed stuck tooting her horn west.
But today–surprise she shifted east!

In these turbulent times, we can't decide
what to do. Things shift quickly.
We lose our sense of direction.

Tolerating Uncertainty

Our goal during this time is to learn to tolerate uncertainty.
Sara Kate McGowan

Late on a cloudy afternoon I don
my long, red cape over my nightgown
and head to the backyard to gulp chi.

This is the first time I have not dressed
during the shutdown. It seems too late now.
When I sit no one can see what's underneath.

It's not likely anyone would notice my disheveled
state. I do wear clean underwear like my mother
always admonished in case of an accident.

My wind-blown hair completes the ultra-
casual look. No butterflies or birds bother
to look at me, but might gossip at a distance.

Two buttercup battalions expand westwards
toward two dandelions escaping near the west fence.
Irises surrender white blooms near the north fence.

I am trying to remain optimistic, to let go and grow,
embrace what could be a cleaner, kinder more
equitable future for this embattled planet.

How tolerant can I be of uncertainty in a world
of constant change, divided intentions? What
impact can I have when shut-in or even when opened?

The thunder-rumble of the neighbor's wheelbarrow intrudes.
He doesn't notice me, as he trudges to his shed. When he's
out of sight, I hightail an exit. My nightgown flaps behind me.

Entering My Garth

What a great word for yard or garden,
like a garden and earth combination.
A new word to play with, to gardon
new observations in my shut-down situation.
　　　When I leave the comfort of my hearth
　　　I have only to go to my garth.

Like a garden and earth combination,
my backyard has grassy and floral components.
Also a sidewalk chunk wall configuration.
I'm one of dandelions' strong proponents.
　　　My garth is a chi-gathering place,
　　　to spin chakras, dream embrace.

A new word to play with, place to gardon
new images with new meanings.
Our garth wishes the mower's pardon
in its relentless, methodical gleanings.
　　　Garth has a hard, raspy sound.
　　　But I like the new earth word I found.

New observations in my shut-down situation
are often found sitting in my garth's chi chair.
As I ponder, meditate on an explanation
for the polluted, viral aspects in our air.
　　　Garth sounds grounded like we are.
　　　We are apart-together, near-far.

When I leave the comfort of my hearth,
I like to contemplate my garth's beauty.
The battering of climate-changing earth,
continues as I'm doing my pandemic duty.
　　　Uncertain times lead to over-hyped fears
　　　which will remain until the atmosphere clears.

I have only to go to my garth,
sun-bake, warm thoughts, breathe deep.
I must endure the mower's swath
as my doubts and misgivings creep.
　　　My garth is my sanctuary, my revival,
　　　as I anticipate the New World's arrival.

In Our Back-garth
            Garth: yard or garden

At three it's a perfect, sunny day.
Birds nap. Bees snooze. No mowers.
Then the wily weeder hauls his bucket,

un-pockets his tools and begins to tug,
dig and hack crab grass. He misplaces
one glove, empties his white pail often.

The watering can is gone. A long
green hose meanders through the
garden, droops from the rock wall.

The results of the butterfly attraction
contest are weeder: 6. Chi-gatherer: 2.
Three flew between us.

We both have close encounters. One
almost abuts his butt. Mine makes a loop
right in front of me within reach.

One blue jay sits on the fence above
two red azalea blossoms poking
through from our side neighbor.

Then the jay flies to a decrepit peach limb,
which struggles to burst feeble small leaves.
Jay goes next door despite our two lush

apple and hazelnut trees eager
for visitors. Two other jays perch in
the peach tree, survey the yard, depart.

One of them just ignores the weeder
below and continues to search for
better pickings in thriving trees.

About a dozen maple seed pods tan
from the back neighbor's gigantic tree.
I doubt the mower allows them to stay.

27

The weeder picks up his tools. I gather
the blue pillow and mobile phone, push
my laden walker toward the house, reflect

he did not breach buttercup boundaries.
Yellow is for caution. It did not work for
dandelions, but maybe these low-liers will live.

Leaf-Shine

The leaves sparkle in spring sun.
Grass briskly prickles with dew.
Rain drains the clouds, brings greening.

Inside peeking outside, the window
frames' outlook like mosaics.
Cataract clearing eyes intensify colors.

In our yard, things are pretty tranquil
in a worrying world. A place of sanctuary.
A place to gather warmth, energize from chi.

It is not quite warm enough to sit outside,
but inside I can get inspired to create
and hope, watch leaf-shine heralding spring.

April is Angel Month

April is Angel Month, part
of the winged-ones wing-ding
in our backyard?

Bees, butterflies, bugs and birds
find this mostly light-filled month
with sunny, warm days inviting.

As I plump my pillow on my chi-
gathering chair in the backyard,
a white butterfly swoops to greet me.

Airlika angel on the hazelnut branch
above me and stationary Tootsie,
the weathervane angel toot silent horns.

I pull up my blue hoodie to protect me
from another nose cancer. With blue
clothing, blue pillow I wish the blues away.

A bee on the dandelion before me makes
touch down twice. Two more puffballs
since yesterday, refreshed by rain.

Red azaleas sneak out of the branches.
Red strawberry leaves foreshadow
what is to come. Apple petals gently fall.

White blueberry and apple blossoms
welcome winged-ones. A second butterfly
flits by. An angel in disguise?

Even angels would love this cloudless
sky and solar-power. Halos would shine.
Wings could cluster, be mistaken for clouds.

Mid-afternoon, the birds have not come
to our organic, motor-less, safe yard. Also
a haven for me. Do I scare them?

Wind-chimes, but no bird chirps. Shiny,
Airlika sways above me. Tootsie, sun bathes.
Cement, prone, Bottom angel chills.

A third butterfly hovers near the fence.
A tiny white moth in the apple canopy.
A distant mourning dove coos.

A fourth butterfly leaves the blueberry bush.
Two neighbors try to start machines which
rat-a-rat-tat. Grating. I'm grateful they don't start.

A fifth butterfly ambles a finale flight.
Is there a bird boycott? Some say they
are angelic messengers to Earthlings.

I can't count on birds. Butterflies so far
this month have been more reliable. Angels
are probably enjoying recognition this month.

When I despair humanity doesn't uplift or
enlighten, somehow I believe in angels,
despite no proof, on just a wing and a prayer.

Rainy Earth Day

April showers bring May flowers is
definitely true this Earth Day. I want
to celebrate nature in my backyard.

As I walk outside I do not hear rain
on the roof. We've had intermittent rain
all day. I think I caught a rain-break.

My blue pillow on my chi-gathering chair
is soaked. I left it outside. I turn it over
and sit down. My bottom's soggy.

Even though light rain falls on my
clothes and joins drops on the grass,
I sit and salute dandelions, red rhodies,

red azaleas, white apple blossoms,
moss on tree trunks, green blades,
winged-ones hiding out to stay dry or nap.

This is their day, but every day really
is Earth Day. My clothes speckle as
rain and wind increase. Wind-chimes chide.

My decorative angels are wet. It is time
to go inside. Such a brief celebration.
Other gatherings and parades are canceled.

I lug the sodden pillow inside to dry. I dampen
an inside chair facing the window wall, place wet shoes
on green slate floor. Rain syncopates on the roof.

I gaze in gratitude at my green, rejuvenating haven.
Despite the pandemic, this April is not like Eliot's
cruelest month. We don't know when that will be.

Endangered Species Day Challenge
  May, 15th 2020   15th Annual

The Endangered Species Coalition
has a species identification challenge
called "What's In My Backyard?"

On May 16th they want us to spend time
in our yard, courtyard or local park to learn
about plant, animal and fungus species there.

But today, like many days I head for my
backyard to deep breathe some chi, seated
in my blue-pillowed chair – today in sun.

I can identify most of what I see, but I'm
no expert on anything. As for endangered—
floral grass enhancements top the list.

Dandelions and buttercups manage
a few survivors each mowing. One tall
dandelion puffball awaits wind in the garden.

No yellow dandelions, but about six
buttercups prevail with azaleas, rhododendrons,
irises, chives, berry blossoms, fruit blooms.

Three white butterflies, but no endangered
monarchs. No bees seen. Plenty of bugs
flying and crawling about. Safely–we're organic.

One sparrow in the blueberry bush. Several
scrub jays visit plum, peach, pear, apple, hazelnut
limbs, rock wall and garden, perch on fence.

Lichen and moss flourish on tree trunks,
rock wall and patio stones. Yard art would
not count, only the living entities do.

Probably the most compromised is the air,
filled with pollutants and viruses. Yesterday,
rain cleansed and nourished the garth.

Humans are an endangered species also.
When they leave, there's no one to count
who is left. No need for the count.

The Day Before Mother's Day

After a Saturday ride checking out
homes with solar panels, gorgeous
irises and other floral delights,

we head home. He to bike ride
and me to chi-gather in my chi chair
in the backyard–84 and sunny.

Two butterflies flitter and flicker,
but do not land. Red rhododendron
blooms fade amid flagrant pink ones.

Two clusters of buttercups migrate
westward, where three puffballs make
a last stand for dandelions.

Airlika, the rusty angel above me
hangs from a hazelnut limb, needs
patina protection before rain rusts more.

Commotion in the hazelnut canopy
distracts me. Two sparrows tweet
and peck at the moss. So energetic.

Several jaunts to the apple branches
and one sparrow peers on our window.
Jays swoop from the roof, scatter yard-wide.

On the surface things seem normal. People
walk groups–some unmasked, many talk
from a social distance, the Saturday Market

still gathers crowds, but we stay in our car.
On our solar survey we meet an owner and
chat about environmental matters, safely.

Visions of splendid irises resonate, as I
wait for our gladiolas to bloom— now tall
green blades. Ants crawl on grass at my feet.

My aeolian hairdo needs combing.
I leave my pillow, as it is astonishingly
sunny and warm, at least until tomorrow.

Fly Aways

Late afternoon on a sunny, seventy
spring day, I move my chi-gathering chair
to a sunny spot and plunk my pillow.

My deep breaths exhale without a mask.
The backyard continues its rhythms
and colorful patterns at a social distance.

A white butterfly flutters by, followed
by another minutes later. No bees.
Fewer bugs than usual. No birds.

It's a dandelion desert. Only a few
seed puffs waft by. Grass cowed,
bent and smooshed.

Airlika angel attached to a hazelnut branch,
Tootsie, the weathervane stuck in west-
south orientation remain doomed not to fly.

The wind chimes have strings attached
as they play with the wind. The pinwheel
could use a plugged-in fan spin.

The watering can rolled to it's side,
spout upward, exposes a black hole.
Perhaps a shelter for birds?

The lichen-encrusted peach tree's
gnarled limbs cling to tiny leaves
struggling from arthritic fingers.

The smallest azalea is a late bloomer,
but musters pink petals to greet the sun
and burgeoning, red-gushing neighbors.

I was about to think I was in a no-fly zone
when two more butterflies swoop the garden
and a blue jay lands and hides in the apple canopy.

My fly-away hair salutes the would be
fliers, the stuck in place–as it blows
gustily, wildly with the wind in fresh air.

Glassed-in Eyes

Sporadic sun struggles to free
from the cloud blockage to splay
inconsistent shadows across the backyard.

I'm too lazy to put on shoes and jacket
for splashes of sun not long enough
to warm my back and shine the yard.

The shadows darken and fade. My chair-
squat and deep breath would not glean enough
rays to reward my efforts. So I sit behind glass.

Protected from wind, uneven weather,
feet on green slate, facing a wall of windows,
I can observe nature without discomfort.

One-half of my glasses lens has been
corrected, reflective of the split weather
clouding clearer vision up close.

The yard appears static with no birds,
butterflies or pinwheel spins. The angels
just hang there not even swaying.

Azaleas and rhododendrons spill onto
the ground but I can't detect their creep.
Leaves barely wave. A landscape painting.

My moods are quicksilver like the sun.
Glimpses of optimism amid grave concern.
As I turn to go in, a blast of sun encourages.

Shifting Attention

A bluetiful jay hops down the rock wall
steps, pecks the lawn, leisurely strolls
near backyard wall and flies to rhododendron.

During my watch five butterflies cruise
the garden. Two dance side by side,
circle each other, before higher flights.

The back-warming sun casts dark shadows.
Tuffs of gray and white seed puffs fluff
around me, I blow them away.

Only three dandelions left. Bees keep away.
In Washington murder hornets decapitate
bees and feed them to their larva. Here?

Bugs whiz by. A fly lands on my thumb.
Unseen bird chirps, wind chimes clang
until droned out by two power mowers.

Both start and stop repeatedly. The eastside
mower angrily shouts to himself and yells at a
red azalea. Luckily there's a fence between us.

Someone to the west whistles for a dog
probably fifteen times for two barks. Four
beeps from a car and I'm done.

A stellar jay swoops in front of me in a cross
lawn flight. A sparrow perches on the back
fence. Do they urge me to stay or go?

I am torn between warm beauty and cold
machine sounds. I pick neither and go
inside to ponder what I do want.

Disappearances

Around two, I head for the backyard,
with newly corrected tinted lens for
my left eye. Much clearer and rosier.

The lawn was mowed this morning.
Three dots of yellow could be
decapitated dandelions, not survivors.

Three butterflies flit across the garden.
Two jays hide in the apple canopy.
One sparrow dives in a rhododendron.

A newly blooming pink azalea separates
a scarlet azalea and rouged rhododendron.
No more petals drop from apple blossoms.

Tiny gray puffs from puffballs and large
white fluffs waft before me to plant
in grass. They arrive from unseen origins.

Shadows crisp and dance. Then
still. Wind chimes whisper and stop.
The pinwheel brushes off breeze.

Wily grass is gone, now monotonously
green and flat. Bees and flies whisk
by me and disappear. Moths keep away.

So many images make a brief appearance.
Masks conceal half a face. We stay put in
our domiciles and when out, social distance.

Handshakes and hugs are past greetings.
Businesses are closed. Events cancelled.
A new normal is emerging. So much change.

As the old world order passes, the new world
more healthy, more sustainable, more just could
be on the horizon. Sometimes, just it let go.

Gentling

Since showers are forecast
for this afternoon, at noon I head
for the backyard to gentle with chi.

My husband moves my chair to a
sunny spot near the hazelnut tree,
facing the eastern half of our yard.

Two butterflies fly in opposite directions.
Four ground-hugging dandelions nestle
near the rock wall. Two other relocate

more safely in the garden near overflowing
red rhododendrons and azaleas spilling
to the earth. Chives stay upright in place.

A gray metal watering can dips its long-
necked spout at the base of a blueberry
bush. From this angle the leaves feather it.

It looks like the wild turkeys ravaging
the north of town— little different coloring
and texture. Luckily inanimate.

Near the filled in wound of the chopped
down cherry tree, two clusters of mushrooms
approach the scar. To mourn?

They are the type like a flattened pancake
with cinnamon on top. They are nubbins now.
I did not expect them so early.

I do not eat mushrooms, but the mangling
mower may not pass them by if they do
not crouch low under their lids. Puffballs bent.

Birdsong stops with a brief mowing next door,
but resumes when quiet returns. The wind-chimes
murmur. Pinwheel and angels remain still.

I deep breathe to spin my chakras, clear out
the kindness, courageous, deadly headlines, to gentle
my turbulence. A stellar jay lands on an apple branch.

It's Rainy

The backyard is soggy,
and dewdrop-shiny.
I will stay inside today.

Behind windows and sock
feet on green slate, I will
be dry, but still chilly.

Drip, drip, drip on canopies.
Raindrops slide down blades.
Dandelions, you don't need sun.

I'm looking in the berry patches,
red rhododendrons and azaleas
inflorescence for dandelions.

Does rain prickle or tickle leaves
and branches? The yard's flora
and fauna must welcome the rain.

Birds get washed off. Butterflies
flick off the drops for exercise.
Airlika angel just gets more rusty.

Pinwheel and wind chimes don't
let rain impede their movement.
However, rain deters mine.

But, we are going for a drive at noon,
grabbing fast food for a change from
cooped-in-ness. Let it rain. Let it rain...

The Watering Can

A gray, metal watering can
hovers over a small blueberry
bush in the garden. Is it empty?

When I first see it from a distance
(over three-times social distance)
it looks like an animal with a snout.

The texture is wrong, so I rule out
a living creature. Some new yard
sculpture I was not informed about?

Moving closer I realize the object
was left behind by an absent-minded
gardener, probably to return to later.

It looks like a mini-bunker with the spout
protrusion, the entry. Not much
of a defense against anything.

In the front yard we do have a line-up
of wild animal yard art. The backyard
gets angels and one metallic bluebird.

I can imagine the watering can into
anything I want, as I thirst for flow
outside the confines of our yard.

The Black Cat

As I sit gathering chi, under
the hazelnut tree, a black cat
strolls slowly through the yard.

It came from the back fence,
looks at me several times
and proceeds out the side yard.

I have not seen a black cat recently
and no cats in that area of the yard.
Cats haven't come by for months.

Black cats have a reputation for
bringing bad luck, as witch companion,
Marvel Comic Book hero.

I try to discern the meaning of
seeing a black cat casually walking
in the backyard. When I go inside

I check the computer. In Vietnam
they kill black cats, to make a paste
to fight off COVID-19 virus.

They slaughter, boil, skin, cook black
cats into a medicine, eaten to prevent
coronavirus with no proven data.

Some people eat cats, dogs and other
animals, but this singling out black cats
for cruel treatment shows their fears.

We blame black bats, but black cats?
Perhaps it is the bad luck idea. But
why would you ingest it?

Lucky for this cat, it is in Oregon. We have
had black cats, as pets, with spots of white.
The wind chills, the sun withdraws shadows.

Is this black cat some kind of omen?
In this pandemic with ensuing uncertainty,
I make no predictions from this black cat.

The Plucky Gardener

On a gusty, overcast afternoon,
I carry my blue pillow to cushion
my chi-gathering chair in the backyard.

A scrub jay hops under red ripe
azaleas to the blushing, gushing
rhododendron. Then humans appear.

Our neighbor rolls a golf ball
to the shed and picks up rake
and sprayers. We briefly greet.

Then the plucky gardener, hauling
a white pail and adze, starts tugging
the grass beards from the rock wall.

Into the garden to pull "weeds" from
the strawberry and blueberry bushes.
He yanks tall blades wherever he can.

We chat about his plucky proclivities
as I sit, with no interest in joining in. He
tosses a stray toy ring back over the fence.

Then he rakes the un-grassed patch
from the filled, chopped cherry tree
remnants and sprinkles some grass seed.

For his convenience he has sprayed
(hopefully organically) brown along the rock
wall and around tree trunks for easy mowing.

His aesthetic is not mine. I do not like
things leavened, color removed from
monotone pallets. I like garish scraggly.

The pinwheel is the wind's puppet
erratically whirling for direction. My
yard angels are unable to guide.

I go inside. Enough grooming. Dandelion
deaths haunt. Enough of this heavy, deadly
world. I crave Dove dark chocolate.

Re-Orientation

During my late afternoon stint
in the backyard, the sun sharpens,
dims and withdraws shadows.

I came to re-acclimate from a nap
where I stand by my long-departed
mother looking at a blank screen.

I do not recall what we talked about,
but out the window I see two white
stupendous spacecrafts. Gi-normous.

In my chi-gathering chair in my familiar yard,
I try to re-connect with this earthly realm. I
see a sparrow poking in a hazelnut niche.

Several sparrows visit this notch. A
nest I can't see? Seed storage? They
fly between apple and hazelnut trees.

The bird traffic is confusing. They fly
so fast I do not know if new birds
have joined the fray or they are returnees.

Scrub jays fly to the plum tree, rhododendrons,
one perches and shimmies on the wooden fence.
Another snacks in the mulch, grass and garden.

A stellar jay lands near the shed behind
my office, passes five starry dandelions lined
up like an honor guard for my dandelion efforts.

A neighbor's pop music blares across spring
air. Occasionally the wind-chimes out-bang
the music, interspersed by mourning doves.

I suppose I belong here quarantined among
free fliers, garish red blooms, clobbered grass,
endangered dandelions, interrupted birdsong.

But I am very happy watching humongous
white spaceships explore the multiverse. In my
multidimensional dreams do I wish to join them?

A Day for White-Bellied Beings

When I carry my blue pillow into
the backyard to chi-gather, I have
to lug the chair off the patio to lawn.

I find a sunny spot, not laced by shadow,
gracing the lawn. Bird shadows fly
over me. I forget to place my pillow.

A small white moth fusses about me,
perhaps checking out if my clothing
is appealing to its taste.

On World Penguin Day, I count
about ten white-crowned sparrows
and a bevy of white butterflies–about nine.

All are solo flights, cosmically-timed,
to criss-cross the northeast corner of
the garden? Butterfly messages from

my departed East coast relatives?
A sparrow climbs the trunk of the
apple tree, then bounces branches.

On the hazelnut limbs sparrows visit
the same notch and explore branches,
firm grip on the thinnest sprigs in gusts.

Nonchalantly, silently, they flit before me,
hide in the foliage and block my view
with branches. I try to catch their movements.

The wind's gusty enough to spin the pinwheel
connecting blue and white lines to whirr
a target. The angel weathervane is unmoved.

All the flying white spots and a few white
speckles from apple and blueberry blossoms.
A few puffballs, but fewer yellow manes flare.

If I reveal my belly, it would be ghostly
white too. So pale I blend with clouds. Flashy,
red rhodies and azaleas blaze by the fence.

With My Better Eye

*My simple understanding is love the planet, ourselves and others. Times of
chaos, look for the helpers- human and angelic.* Barbara Poulsen

On a fair-to-middling mid-afternoon,
I plunk my blue pillow on my chilled chi-
gathering chair, planted on patio stones.

Too overcast to move the chair into sun.
The sky is foggy-gray, with not enough
sun-backing for shadows.

I rely on my better eye to survey
my surroundings, as I wait new
lenses for my glasses.

The later-blooming apple tree casts
her white petals west into a oasis edged
by two dandelions and two puffballs.

A widdershins wind blew a few petals
East. No gusts to spin pinwheel, jangle
wind-chimes, sway yard angels.

Today no butterflies, but birds. Two
stellar jays in the apple and hazelnut
trees, swoop in with a flare then leave.

Two tiny birds prefer to ignore me in the
hazelnut tree before me. Black heads and
backs, white head-stripe and belly.

Red azaleas and rhododendrons flash
against the fence. A neighbor clangs
a wheelbarrow into his shed, sneezes.

My dandelion count is disappointing,
but several puffballs are encouraging.
I wish we could maintain this temporary

wilder and cleaner world. My hair wind-dried.
I go inside. When my glasses return, will I
see the world through sun-tinted lenses?

A Sun Dance

*Take earth for your own large room and the floor of the earth carpeted with sunlight
and hung round with silver wind as your dancing place.* May Swenson

Late afternoon on a chilly, overcast day,
I haul my aching limbs into the backyard
to energize by chi-gathering, seated in my chair.

Wind and solar power weak. The shadow-less,
motionless yard needs to enliven. I wonder
if I should choreograph a sun dance.

Maybe the wind will accompany with wind-chimes.
Perhaps the birds will chirp a chorus.
Deep plane drone provide bass?

Come on jays leave the power line and
bounce some branches. Butterflies you are
too late to rehearse. Bees sway flowers.

Apple petals pirouette to the dance floor.
Elderly puffballs and dandy dandelions have
plenty of partners. Great backup dancers.

Green blades of grass and floral stalks
are ready to rock and roll. Red azaleas
and newly emerging red rhodies are dazzlers.

Wallflower, stuck in place Tootsie, the
angel weathervane needs a divine kick
to get into gear to move. Pinwheel, twirl.

Above me, Airlika angel looks rusty
below the hazelnut branch. She is not
empowered by wind to move side to side.

So I have to conjure them into motion.
Daydream dance them into my sun dance
which enlightens us all. Fairies can join in.

A dandelion pairs with my chair leg. I have
not danced–except maybe whirl my chakras.
A brief shot of sun with faded shadow indicates

maybe tomorrow the sun will come whether
I can dance for it or not. I can still choreograph
a corona-inspired dance for the sun's corona.

Traipsing Terrain with Binoculars

With binoculars in tow for the first time,
I venture into the backyard, plunk my
blue pillow on my chi-gathering chair.

Perfect spring day, high-sixties, sunny
breezy enough for floral wind dances,
jazzy wind-chimes and pinwheel spins.

But weathervane angel Tootsie does not
budge–toots west. Airlika angel on hazelnut
branch above me shines in midday sun.

With my cataract-cleared eye, I squint
at the yard. Red, three-lobed leaves emerge
from the strawberry patch. One much larger.

The lupin are defoliating. Nineteen
puffballs disintegrating. Fourteen
yellow dandelions intact–glowing.

Sun crisps shadow edges. Bees in canopies. Through
the back fence slats, I see slices of a neighbor, who
issues commands and pets his black and white dog.

The first faithful white butterfly appears, followed
by a second who seems to scribble a message
which my old-slow eyes can't see or read.

Then a third butterfly–an angelic SOS?
When the fourth comes I decide they
are substituting for the absent birds.

I take the binoculars on and off. Smile
at the lone dandelion among fallen apple
petals social-distancing from me.

I drop my pen. Can't find it. The phone rings
inside, followed by a nearby siren. Seems my
un-hassled time is up. I re-cap the binoculars.

I went to the backyard with heavy, deep sighs.
I return to my home with chi-filled, deep breaths–
uplifted, as the shadows shift, sun illuminates horizon.

Spring Re-wilding

Midday, I go into the backyard
to sun-dry my hair, loop chi
and commune with the wild ones.

A sunny, warm day, perfect to lure
the hibernating creatures to join
others animals reclaiming national parks.

Sheep have invaded towns, foxes, wolves,
coyotes, rabbits scour empty malls. Tourists'
and shoppers droppings are missed. Free to roam.

A groundhog ate pizza outside a window
as a confined dog watched. Our neighbor's
dog paces beside the fence, eyeing our yard?

A bonanza day for butterflies. I spy
seven white ones flittering all over.
Two meet mid-air and dance.

In our organic, pesticide-free yard,
the bees, decimated by half since
first Earth Day, have free reign.

Bees probe the apples blossoms. One
bee rests on a fallen petal. I sit
surrounded by petals- grass dandruff.

The petals each have their own spot.
Do they aim or have some innate distancing
guidance system. I'm not petal-touched.

Some tiny birds in the blueberry bush-
bigger than a butterfly, but smaller than
little brown jobbers. New dark entities?

The Stellar Jays swoop from the roof.
They land in branches–briefly. One splays
in a belly flop in the garden, wings spread.

Above me on the hazelnut branch, metal
angel, Airlika's left-side looks polished by
sun-glow. Webs shine in rock wall crevices.

The sturdy dandelions survive and thrive.
Proud puffballs ready for wind-seeding.
Red azaleas adorn the flashy fence.

My towel-tossed hair is dry. I go inside
to comb my hair and my thoughts— out
of control, wild-ing during this quarantine.

Gratitude

Mid-afternoon when my co-quarantine mate
returns from his bike ride, I don my red cape,
carry my blue pillow to my chi chair to deep breathe.

Apple petals speckle the lawn. I can conjure
them as albino dandelions. Wind gusts splatter
white flecks all over the flat grass.

I did spot seven dandelion survivors of recent
mowing and the puffball blew its head off,
touches of sun amid petal snow flurry.

Above me on the hazelnut branch Airlika,
the rusty angel sways with sun-glistened face.
A lady bug, a blood spot on a small leaf.

Bees on the blooming blueberry bush, but
not on the two late-bloomers bushes. A jay plops
in the same garden plot and spreads wings.

Just two Stellar jays today. One on the power
line. One prostrate in the garden gathering
solar power? Resting? Eliminating?

One makes a pit stop at the peach tree
which is encrusted, barren, barely upright.
Stooped, it looks like a skinny witch.

A small white moth appears first. Then a
faithful white butterfly, followed later by a
briefer bonus flyby. Moth eyeing my cape?

Are birds and butterflies inspirited by beloveds
from beyond to encourage us, uplift our spirits?
If so, I wonder who stopped by today?

Tall grasses spill through rock wall. Red
azalea blooms are sparking up the fence.
Pinwheel spins like wheel of fortune.

There has been some good news. The pipeline
was halted. Masks ordered by grandson arrived
with no English on package. My favorite color blue.

I pulled down my sleeping mask after a nap
and discovered if pulled down it could do
in a pinch. But black is not uplifting.

My friend is fourteen days without a fever
and recovering from COVID-19. It is a
cloudless, warming splendiferous day.

At times I squint to see through my
cataract-free eye for the cataract-filled
eye is blurry. I prefer to see clearly.

I walk to the wall to look at tiny yellow
flowers in the top tier grass. My friend
used to yank them out when she visited.

I laugh as I think they are beautiful, like
dandelions in training. As I head inside I am
grateful to be in a safe, nature-touched place.

On a Wing and a Prayer

A newspaper columnist suggests
stay-in-place participants go outside
in two fifteen minute segments.

Carrying my blue pillow I go into
the backyard for a half-hour chi
session under 70's clear sky.

Sun pelts my un-hooded pate
and red-caped back on this
cloudless, warming spring day.

Many gray puffballs go to seed
naturally. Bees visit the yellow
crop momentarily free from mower.

White blooms on blueberry bushes
and ground-hugging strawberries compete.
Blueberry blossoms more than strawberry.

Above me in the hazelnut tree a bird splat
on Airlika angel's rusty neck. Nearby apple
blossoms flake wind-plucked petals into grass.

Bees prefer the apple blooms over
dandelions, it seems. No birds or
butterflies in this breezy scene.

Distant chirps. Out of sight planes.
Wind-chimes dance music for fairies
dancing in another dimension?

A jay on the power line flies to neighbor's
yard. I extend my chi time ten minutes
in hopes of seeing my faithful white butterfly.

Just as I was about to return inside, disappointed,
a solo show by a white butterfly renews my
hope for a less turbulent, dark world.

Many of us are winging it together. I'll
look for the good news and for renewal
when I sit looping chi, connecting realms.

Late-Afternoon Backyard Haiku

shadows clutter lawn
an overlay of darkness
dims dandelion shine

puffballs await blowhard
winds to shake seeds free
sturdy stems bend

bees on apple blossoms
sweeter than dandelions
or less likely detected

two stellar jays nip
at struggling peach tree
siren warns them away

one jay darts between
apple and hazelnut trees
above me claims domain

trees encrusted with moss
and lichen still produce leaves,
blossoms despite tough husks

rough edged rock wall
softens with drooping grasses
spider webs with dew

Outside On Easter

When the wily weeder returns
from adzing the fence weeds,
I take my cue, put on my shoes,
carry a phone, so he can bike ride.

In my haste I by-pass my pillow,
so I sit on my hard chi chair. As
I open the back door, a jarred jay
jumps from the garden and flies away.

Overheard bees in apple blossoms.
I whisper, "Go low." I fought for these
dandelions sprawled au natural
in about the same positions as yesterday.

Brown birds nip blueberry bushes.
Two white butterflies from the East.
One white butterfly from the West.
Choreography on the wind.

Two planes do not leave contrails.
A buzz saw stutters. Wind-chimes
jangle. A siren wails. A reminder
of the harsh reality beyond these confines.

A humongous next door dog pushes
his nose through the fence. We stare
silently. I revisit dandelions, florets of sun
radiating the yard. Some puffballs poofed.

About social distance above me a jay swoops
telling me my time's up and my presence
interrupts afternoon snacking. I abandon my
attempts for lofty thoughts, higher thinking.

I am an outsider this Easter, but we are
all together in our confinement. I hear
multiple voices nearby. They are not
abiding the gathering ban. They laugh.

On bike rides, he sees several violators
breathing closely. Can we flatten the curve?
Will we soon work together for the resurrection
of an equitable, sustainable, kind, new world?

Transitions

The Passover Holiday is literally a story of going from confinement to freedom and from winter to spring. Benj Paser

Many Passover and Easter gatherings
will be held by screen or postponed.
Many people will be confined at home.

This Good Friday is sunny
so I will go into the backyard
from confinement inside, draw chi.

Within the confines of the backyard
free-growing grass–clipped. Dandelions
beheaded. Victims of a grim reaper.

The dandelions and I are victims of a
late spring and forces we have no control
over. I face virus. They face a control freak.

He prefers to be called
the Fiskar Guillotiner
wielding Adam's adze.

He calls me the Chi
Gatherer. I prefer
Dandelion Advocate.

On this shiny Good Friday,
I witness the prostrated lawn
squiggling to be free.

One friend says the dandelions
are going to Jesus. In my lawn
that's unlikely. Maybe brighten sun?

Perhaps by Easter the lawn
will resurrect until the next mow down.
We don't know when Corona passes over.

Thinking of Thoreau

When I head to the backyard
to sun-dry my hair and inhale
chi, I think of Thoreau.

Henry isolated at Walden Pond.
I have my backyard. He went into
Concord to have dinner with friends.

He could have visitors. I cannot
go into town or have visitors.
It's been weeks. Maybe weeks more.

Through the fence slats I spy a sleeveless
tee-shirt, a back-neighbor scooping dog poop,
putting it into a plastic bag, silently.

Henry could converse with nearby Irish
railroad workers, gossip in town, his was
not an enforced isolation. A self-quarantine.

Henry was in constructive solitude.
He chose his boundaries, unlike the
corona captives confined today.

Henry wrote his field research,
philosophical and autobiographical
entries in his journal. I write poems.

He mentions his library has 900 volumes
over 700 of them his. I far surpass this.
I almost double his 44-year life-span as well.

This sunny 70s day with cottony clouds
chugging south, I scout for dandelions.
One magnificent puffball–about 9 inches tall!

About four more puffballs and about 19
yellow youngsters. Apple blossoms explode
from the branch above me. Birds flit among

the blueberry and rhododendron bushes.
One agitated jay rushes small birds from
the blueberry bush and dashes away.

Then a white butterfly finally made an
appearance, tranquilly fluttering before
me. I always look for butterflies too.

The roof shadow creeps closer to my chair.
My wind-tussled hair dried. I should head inside.
I resist shaking the trembling tall puffball

to free the seeds. The wind nibbles at the
gray-white head, like mine. Perhaps a gust
with gusto will release seeds' containment.

Henry was into social-distancing when he
was irritated at humanity. He retreated to
his shed, his refuge, his retreat, by choice.

Henry was cooped up for two years in self-
education, unbridled reading, clarified thinking.
I hope my confinement isn't that long, but productive.

In Chrysalis Mode

Chrysalis just hang out there, isolating itself from the world and changing in ways it can never understand. Chris Corrigan

For rebirth and renewal to take place,
a period of hibernation and darkness
must happen first? Why?

This Maundy Thursday as I look
at the destruction of the dandelions
by the Mower Mangler, I ask why?

Can I hope for an Easter resurrection
for them like the white butterfly who
flits over their loss of landing pads?

The equal opportunity weed-wiper
also wields toothy "Andy" adze, to
dig out any oopart in the lawn.

He does not get praise from me
for his edging, bland, boring lawn.
But he's puffed this Sheer Thursday.

He is in control of his weedy domain.
Scraggly grass can get too tall for easy
mowing, dandelions take grass room.

His arguments do not soothe me.
I'll sit amid devastation while still cocooning.
I carry my blue pillow like a bruise.

Pauses of Sun

The sun comes out and then hides and sometimes it rains or sprinkles. Sort of like life. Anne Yates

Mid-afternoon the sun returns
pauses of light. The shadows
darken over the backyard lawn.

Will I go outside as I planned?
I don my red cape, but hesitate
putting on my shoes. Its cold out.

Instead I sit with an afghan on my
lap, peer through windowed walls
at raindrops glistening grass.

Mowing has been postponed due
to rain showers. Dandelions reflect
the sun. Wind-chimes play lullabies.

The pinwheel splays itself to sun,
gently drying. One yard angel sways
on a branch. Another sunbathes.

In my dream last night I was in a sunny,
desert landscape part of a team to upgrade
and renovate buildings at an undisclosed place.

We boarded a windowless capsule to tunnel
deep into Earth or to another dimension. A cluster
of blah brick buildings- a religious compound in shutdown?

We had a young Dutch-cut blonde tour guide.
The place was deserted-sun-braised. Barren
no matter where you looked. Apocalyptic.

The guide took us to the back of a church.
A dribbly-nosed, feverishly, red-faced pastor
named Mr. Righteous thrust fliers at me.

He was a contagion to his congregation. I
foisted the fliers on a parishioner and left
the scene, waking in bed near sun-blazed window.

But the sun did not stay for long as showers
commenced throughout the day. During this pause
my husband returned from a sunny bike ride.

He reported it was cold and windy.
So I moved to my office, my sanctuary,
brightened by artificial light.

Tomorrow I will wait for sun pauses
and attempt again to gather chi, sitting
in my chi chair under the hazelnut tree.

A Soggy Day

It's a soggy day. The backyard
is mushy, greening lushly.
Unrelenting gray skies scowl.

I resist putting on shoes to moosh
through the grass to my wet chi chair.
Rain-breaks are brief, unpredictable.

Through a wall of windows framing
the currently wind-less scene, I hear
distant bird chirps, but no wind-chimes.

The pinwheel looks like a striped flower.
Yard angels just hang out, take a nap.
No thirsty essences to be seen.

Through the gap-toothed fence,
the back neighbor's light sparkles
on a sun-less day. Some tiny shine.

A scrub jay jitters through hazelnut branches,
lands to parade at the patio's edge, flies to roof
and power line–uncertain where to land.

Does the jay greet the inanimate metal blue
jay, staked in the patio pavings? Did the jay
notice Bottom, concrete angel glistening in rain?

A whisk of wind spins the pinwheel, too wimpy
to jangle the wind chimes. I will not wait
for weather changes to go outside.

Snug in my inside chair, under the afghan,
I observe window frames, creating still lives.
For a while I am not engulfed by the world.

Gearing Up

During a rain respite, benign drops spitting
at us, my husband hauls a ladder
to a hazelnut limb to re-hook Airlika.

The rusty angel was dangling upside
down by her feet, wind-dancing over
my chi chair. Now she toots her horn flying.

I foray in full protective gear into the backyard.
Shoes on for the first time in days. Thick, white
fleecy jacket and hood. Red cape shawled.

It is overcast and sixty, but I look like
a bloody wooly mammoth about
to embark into the Arctic.

I carry my blue pillow to cover the wet chair
seat, the arms polka-dotted with rain.
Airlika looks straight west above me.

A dandelion social distances beside me.
Others also appear to spread out. A plump
puffball shivers in gusts about to fill the gaps.

One tiny dandelion seed lands on my red cape.
I flick it to the ground. I do my deep breaths,
try to loop chi, razzle-dazzle my chakras.

Shadows sprint across the lawn as a hint
of sun. Bird-shadows speckle sky. Raindrops
sparkle in the grass until it clouds over again.

Wind-gusto spins the pinwheel and clangs
the wind-chimes. Tootsie, the weathervane angel
remains unmoved, refuses to budge.

A few bugs. For awhile we seem in the bird's
flight pattern. Four in succession land on the power
pole, several balance on the power line.

Two birds, probably jays, exchange spots.
One on the power line flies down as another
flies up from the rhododendron.

I decide to go inside when the shadows
fade, don't shade. I watch three small birds
in the hazelnut branches, flitting about.

My husband comes out to check on me as it
has been over an hour. We study hazelnut
birds and pronounce them sparrows, tentatively.

We do inside. I shed my protective gear,
layer by layer. I kick my shoes off again,
wriggle my toes, thaw under my red cape.

Sitting outside and inside our fifth acre
is all the 3D reality I see. News is pressed
onto pages and screens, as we flatten the curve.

Everyone I know is quarantined–several sick.
One with COVID-19. We do not know when our
vistas will expand. I'm gearing up for the long haul.

When the Sun Don't Shine

A gray pall hovers over the backyard.
Light rain splatters the window, three
streams of water overflow from the gutter.

A wind twirls the pinwheel, but not enough
gusto to tingle the wind-chimes, or provoke
the dandelion puffball brigade to reseed.

A bird on the power line chirps as another
bird flies by. The bird, beam gymnast or
trapeze artist, walks the wire with flare.

When the gutter gushes stream over
the backdoor and outdoor light, I tell
my husband who is not pleased to know it.

Through the back fence after days of absence,
the orangish light returns to sparkle through the
slats. Same spot. Did neighbors shorten a timer?

My husband hustles to the mini-waterfalls,
gutter trowel in hand, hauling a ladder. He scoops
the goop. Mucky wet leaves fling to the ground.

I watch, mentally balancing the ladder. He was
glad to clean up the mess. I must admit I liked
the drip. I observe a mostly motionless scene.

Rain-shine does not lure me to my chi chair
like sunshine does. Behind the glass, I cuddle
in my red cape, social distancing, staying in.

My metal chi chair chills without me. I deep
breathe to balance my chakras. Looping chi,
cosmos to earth core, faces many barriers.

Contact in this viral, hand-washing, non-touching
world forces more introspection, a chance
to clean up your act and unfurl positive change.

Criticizing their Stewards

Notes from our backyard entities convention:

"The arborist whacked my trunk
into ugly scabs", said the spruce.

"I was lopsided for a year", said
the apple tree "before they balanced me".

"I'd like more wiggle and stretch time
before mowings", said a grass blade.

"A crop circle or a new mowing pattern,
would be nice." said another blade.

"I'm insulted he considers me a weed. She
adores me as a drop of sun," said a dandelion.

"I'm grateful they did not chop me down like
the cherry tree as I struggle," said the peach tree.

"At least we are all organic and not inhaling
toxins," said the hazelnut tree.

"I need oiling or something, my joints don't
seem to move," said Tootsie, the angel weathervane.

"I dangle head down since my head hook unhooked.
I'd like to swing more like a cradle again", said Airlika,
the rusty angel.

"I'm at the will of the wind. Can't plan ahead for
a respite, time to gather my thoughts," said the pinwheel.

"As another entity they consider inanimate, I compose
music. Inanimates have consciousness too." said
one rod of a wind-chime.

"As part of a gap-toothed fence, more critters pass
through, despoil our footings, I wish they'd repair
our slats," said a leaning fence slat.

"Moss covers us patio pavers like the trees and rock
walls. We are warmed, protected, thank you moss,"
said a comforted paver.

"I weather all storms, cradle leaf deposits
lying on my back on a blue table" said Bottom,
concrete angel. "Like perennials I have a long
view of things, like the fences and walls marking
our place. The Smiths may be elderly, but he
tries to sustain and maintain us. She is our watcher,
praising our efforts with gratitude."

Lull in Storms

Mid-afternoon in the lull between
storms, my husband risks a bike ride.
I stay inside and observe the backyard.

Through glass, in filtered air, the lull
brings the backyard to a standstill.
No wind-chimes jingle or pinwheel spin.

A steady stream of rain dribbles from
the gutter outside the back door. The yard
is drenched. I'll cuddle in my red cape inside.

No birds flyover or land in the mossy branches.
Rusty angel Airlika dangles from the hazelnut
limb, pointing at my empty, cold, wet, black chair.

Bottom, the prone concrete angel is taking
a bath in his table tub. Tootsie, the angel
weathervane is oblivious to wind.

I strain to check up on dandelions, but they
seem in remission. Lupin look lush and
white blossoms on the pear tree–profuse.

I hear the rain on the skylight, but the biker
appear undeterred from his hour trek. I
deferred my backyard chi time–deep breathe.

I sigh. Exhale sadness and inhale hope,
pretend self-quarantine is a staycation.
The wet biker returns, refreshed and safe.

Gray Skies

Gray skies scowling at me
nothing but gray skies do I see...
It is three o'clock, decision time.

My husband's home from a bike ride.
I have staffed the phone. Now he showers
to rid himself of world's detritus.

I sit with lap blanket facing the damp
chilly backyard behind glass.
The morning sun has vanished.

I waited too long to go out. Now
I can see a blue jay grub the garden
way apart from even social distance.

When a peephole of sun splays
a faint shadow across the lawn,
I am briefly hopeful if I wait, maybe...

At least a few jays fly by, a rustle
of tiny brown birds in the bushes.
Most movement is wimpy from pinwheel,

limp wind-chimes, stagnant yard angels.
The gaps in the leaning wooden back fence
droop more visibly. We do not own it to fix.

I await updates on friends and family
facing various health and financial challenges.
I'm stuck inside and unable to visit them.

I was really hoping the morning blue skies
would last longer. Tomorrow, whenever
the sun appears, I'm venturing outside.

I'll lasso some chi, chuff my chakras,
send hopeful vibes into the universe.
Until then, I'll high-five and fingerprint glass.

Five O'Clock Shadow

Between rain bursts, the sun
casts a 5:00 shadow across
the green stubble of the backyard.

I am exercising my birthday privilege
to view the scene through two panes
of glass, past a shaded enclosed room.

I have my red cape and lap quilt.
I am dry and warm as I peruse
the framed darkening landscape.

Dandelions shelter in place within
their seeds. Those who burst free
of lock down, social distance across lawn.

Wind-wriggling, spindly hazelnut limbs
sway rusty, angel Airlika who honks
her hollow horn over my empty chair.

Tootsie, the weathervane angel
stolidly toots her slender horn northwest
beside our occasionally agitated pinwheel.

The wind chimes clang loudly when
provoked. Then I spot a yellow spark on
the back fence. My husband does not see it.

He reports a neighbor's backyard light
might sparkle between the fence slats.
I'll conjure an angel's flashlight.

I keep looking for birds. Can't see any
creatures lurking in the bushes or trees.
Too early for dinner, too late for snacks?

A global chill is keeping us shut in. Breaths
of fresh, healthy air–treasured. I relish phone,
paper and on-line contacts until we can touch.

Between Storms

Between storms, I leave my computer
and move to gaze through the large glass
door overlooking our indoor room to backyard.

The lifted accordion shade, keeping cold and sun
outside, allows me to view the backyard from
the living room in comfort. I grab a chair and blanket.

A row of small sunflower decals at eye level
keeps me sitting tall. They protect us from crashing
through the glass. In an enclosed outdoor room,

a spiral, dowel Christmas tree with wooden ornaments
blocks the living trees. My blue pillow on the table
will not join the drying metal chi chair outside today.

Through the wall of windows I can see my chair
under the hazelnut tree. A splendid stellar jay
struts just above where I usually sit, taunts me.

Gray clouds show blue sky patches and white
clouds above the trees, cast occasional faint
shadows on the lawn. The pinwheel limply spins.

I cannot hear the wind-chimes or bird chirps.
All is quiet until my husband reports from
a bike ride. Only a grocery store was busy.

Dandelions seem reluctant to spread in increasingly
unruly lawn. This mid-afternoon I did not want to don
shoes and coat for a chilly, damp, backyard sojourn.

I am a comfortable observer during uncomfortable times.
I try to select my viewpoints. I put down my reading
glasses and with my cataract-free eye see more clearly.

Cloud-Sprinters

A cold front and rain
thrust the clouds east
across the window frame.

Rapidly their contours
change, the metamorphoses
and color shifts keep me entranced.

The blue sky, blurs gray,
cloudless, then bunched and
layered. Bumpy and smooth.

The sky-sculptor struggles
with its muse to shape the day
until camouflaged by night.

Branches sketch dark lines
below the cloud canvas.
I debate when a hiatus

will let me go outside to sit.
But the grass is damp, air is cold.
My rain-dripped chair drizzles chi.

Behind Windows

Sitting behind a wall of windows
I observe the newly mowed backyard,
uniformly green, same height conformity.

Apple petals mulched into the grass.
Puffballs aided in depositing seed.
Dandelions shredded to the earth.

He does not mow the garden. Red
azaleas lure me to come into the yard.
Along the fence, are they stop lights?

Red rhododendrons camouflage the fence,
but the defenseless lawn was chopped
into bio-bits. There is enough dying.

Maybe tomorrow the renewal will start.
I just can't re-stake my chi chair in such
destruction today. I'll deep breathe inside.

Sure the allure of the burgeoning garden
is a distraction. I could focus there and
avoid the tidy, clipped yawn of lawn.

But I need to encompass the whole
of reality surrounding me, try to keep
safe and protect others inside.

Maybe I have been behind windows
too long. Shut-in from the elements
for weeks with brief backyard forays.

When windows open and we go outside,
to breathe cleaner air will be a celebration.
But for today I keep pain outside panes.

Spring Quarantine

Trying to predict the future
is like trying to drive down a country road
at night with no lights
while looking out the back window.

Peter Drucker

Wintery Spring

In the midst of winter, I found within me, an invincible summer. And that makes me happy. For it says that no matter how hard the world pushes against me, there's something strong — something better, pushing right back.
Camus quote from *The Plague* sent by Kathy Ross

This morning as the rain returned, after
sunny, greening, springing days, Oregon
joined the shut-down, shelter in place order.

Only essential businesses are to remain open.
Parks are closed. Art and sport venues closed.
Health, delivery, grocery, take-out food workers-stay.

I listen to the rain splatter on the skylight,
watch rain drip from my backyard chi chair,
I know rain is essential so I'll adjust.

My plan to sit outside foiled. I delay dressing
until after lunch. Another rescheduled day
in self-quarantine. Screens and newspapers inform.

The Olympics in Japan postponed. Italy shows
some sign of improving. New hot spots emerge.
In the neighboring county— a viral death.

We are a few days past the spring equinox.
This winter of our discontent has a long way
to pass through spring for the hope of summer.

In the kindness and courage of others, I see
the brighter side of this pandemic, we connect
and touch in new ways. Pollution lessens.

But global leadership needs to address the suffering
from all perspectives. Trump should not appoint
a trophy hunter advocate to protect our environment.

Spring break means close more beaches so
partiers do not infect others when they return home.
We learn we are all in this together—at least some do.

As we contemplate new ways of thinking and acting,
perhaps an inner spark of light will guide our way
for a new dawn after a still star-string night.

Showering in Quarantine

Why am I inside in my claustrophobic
shower stall when I could be re-purposing
the incessant, intermittent rain
into an outdoor shower?

Instead of gazing through glass
at my backyard, yearning to sit
amid nature to chug some chi
and empower my chakras,

I could be tiptoeing through dandelions,
a naked, fubsy, female, flapping flab
flailing a washcloth when not scrubbing,
air-drying slowly in the cleansing rain.

No one goes in the backyard but us.
Everyone is cloistered, busy with
their version of a staycation. But
it is still too chilly, so I stay inside.

Not that I am tempted to shower
outside even when not in quarantine.
I just imagine an excuse to sit outside
soaking warm sun, rejuvenating.

So as I scrub in my inside shower,
sit on the bottle-holding bench fantasizing
such a scene, I am glad my imagination
is not reality. I have been inside too long?

After toweling and dressing, I return to
my inside chi chair. The overcast sky
delays my husband's bike ride, but
the backyard thrives with the showers.

Gently Falls the Rain

The Earth is quieter and less polluted
due to less emissions from shut down
people, staying in place.

In the wild west we are taming our
excessive appetites, but the crazy
eight mid-west states remain unbridled.

I ramble around my disbanded Corona coven,
sit inside the glass door with its row of sunflowers
to remind people it is there and to ponder exiting.

When we had more grubby hands about,
fingerprints imprinted the glass, but now
we are to wash our hands. Notice sunflowers.

I am noticing dandelions to celebrate them
tomorrow on their special day. In the front
yard they are social distancing gracefully.

In the backyard I spy four low-lying blooms
and two hugging the stone wall. Not too many
to compose dandy-lines in their honor.

It is a rainy, chilly, late spring. Few birds stay
to snack, most stay briefly to catch their breath.
More birds perch and peck in more abundant yards.

The rain gently fall, almost invisible. The yard
angels, pinwheel, wind-chimes are still. We
all wait for a cleansing breeze to breathe safely.

My Staycation

I am sheltering in place, social
distancing, washing hands,
staying in self-quarantine.

I am trying to view the situation
as a vacation, a time to relax,
free creativity, contact without touch.

All the isolating terms due to the
coronavirus renew worries, fears
for others, feel sadly heavy-handed.

But in my green oasis, I can soak
in the intermittent sun, escape screens
when I can no longer take dark barrage.

I can only sign so many petitions, endure
so much news, tolerate misguiding leadership
just so long until I go on staycation mode.

Some solace comes with solitude,
reducing exposure to media's manipulation.
There are no meetings or events to go to.

My mindset is to remind myself I am retired,
elderly. It's my time to create what I choose.
I'll help others if I can. But I'm on staycation.

Social Distancing Playing Scrabble

One of our Scrabble players suggested
playing Scrabble outside six feet apart.
It was a joke but a fun challenge
to how this could be done.

We would have to go up to the board,
one at a time, place the tiles and return
to our socially distant seat. Be careful
to walk straight and not breathe near anyone.

We could take our turn, not knowing what
was put on the board. We would have to
place all the tiles, not touching for pick-up.
Maybe on another table to avoid contact?

All this would have to be carefully coordinated.
We would be within voice range. If we relied
on a smart phone, I would be in a pickle. I am
still learning. Might up my curve by necessity?

Some in the group play on-line with strangers.
One suggested we find a way to do so with
our group. I'm not the techie to figure it out.
I'll just take a hiatus from Scrabble for now.

My mother's name Honey appears in games
of Cooperative Scrabble. I hope she sees
from beyond we are not playing, so not excluding
her from our word-play. She watches anyhow?

Would we sanitize the tiles before and after
we play? Squirt the board with sanitizer? This
could be quite a project. Imaginative Scrabble
could be a real set-up, take down hazard.

Imagination can create new ways to play,
to conjure a world from our dreams. I will
word-play with other patterns, scrabble letters
and place them in new contexts in new games.

Corona Cocoon

Keep diving inward into the corona cocoon. Barbara Poulsen

This morning a chilly sun
poked my lallygagging body
from the bed to dress for the day.

Before noon the rain returned.
Now I am waiting until afternoon
when we are promised sun again.

I want to sit in the damp backyard,
pillow-protect my chair, draw chi. These
sittings are my only excursions outside.

My husband with surgical precision
returns from errands, sanitizes goods,
all he touched and then self with a shower.

He ordered groceries on-line. There is
a week's delay in pick-up. He feels
responsible for the world's burdens.

I am lightening up. My motto:
Better six feet apart than six feet under.
Reduce news programs, seek comedies.

To me the pandemic is indicative of imbalance
in the world. We need to be better planetary
stewards and for each other. Time to work together.

I do not understand Earth laws and why
such darkness is allowed to cocoon us,
to flatten the curve of our potential.

I witness all the adaptations and innovations
the coronavirus unfolds. Fear the dangers
to the health care providers and lack of supplies.

We seem to be trying to balance. I will remain
in my cocoon until I grow some wings to fly,
keep the best of the old and embrace the new.

Returning Refrigerator Magnets

After a recent cleaning of the fridge front,
all the magnets were put in a box-stored.
The white-faced door looked pale, colorless.

Usually amid the angels, animals, tourist sites
and event magnets are newspaper clippings, comic
strips, photos, poem posters, postcards, Obama.

Entombed for months, I missed their spots
of color and word-play. Now that I am sheltering
in place, I have time, no excuse not to rescue them.

I created a folder for the excess, to reduce clutter.
I will exchange them for those in the spotlight
when we either wash the door or I change places.

One by one I found a spot for the magnets.
They may hold different articles. Some hold
medical information for easy access.

I filled the barren plane, remembering where
I bought them, if they were gifts. Some origins
fade from memory. I appreciate designs and color.

I live in a mini-museum filled with thousands
of seasonal and perennial creatures. Angels
roost everywhere. I had neglected these magnets.

In this time of isolation these light spots console.
Now a few more on the refrigerator-more the merrier.
A black jointed, lanky body can move positions.

This gender-less, hairless flat form changes postures
according to the whim of a passerby. I position the
limbs as a graceful dancer ready to dance.

April Fools Day

Weather casters predicted sun to appear
around four. No joke. It did, prompting
my husband's daily bike ride.

Incessant rain is hail in some places.
It is too cold for me to venture from
beyond the wall of windows.

My daily vigil is performed without
my red cape or shoes. But an afghan
with loopy holes covers my legs.

Sharp, dark shadows yawn across
uniformly mowed boring lawn.
No remains of dandelions.

He insists on manicuring the yards.
The front yard has abundant dandelions.
They migrate sparsely to the backyard.

No one but us has been in the backyard
in months. Since we switched to electric,
not even a gas meter reader. It's capped.

Shadows fade with fickle clouds.
Pinwheel's and wind-chimes tempo
changes at whim of the wind.

We are self-quarantining. I welcome
seeing waves of freedom, wildness.
Not a fan of clipping nature.

He is proud of his handiwork. I am annoyed.
But why should I whine when the unruly,
traumatic world is jut out of sight–suffering?

My solace is chilled, darkened, dampened.
How long must I soul-dig inside? They insist
we will get through this together. How and when?

Behind a Wall of Windows

Beyond my windows some say
coronageddon or coronapocalyse
exhales on us to inhale.

Some say, save masks for health
care workers. Make your own mask.
Don't breathe on or touch anyone.

Some cheer walker-gawkers with chalk
art on sidewalks, teddy bears in windows,
uplifting signs, Christmas decorations,

sing to medical staff from balconies,
create viral videos, exercise and dance
in their yards—six feet apart.

We are to pull together in spirit not contact.
We are to self-quarantine for protection.
Stay home if we can. Order in.

But then there are workers who can't
stay home, they deliver goods, perform
essential services at great risk.

As I sit inside, watching the backyard
cleanse in rain, I am thinking of those
beyond my windows–unseen, untouched.

Manifesting My Cloister

During my confinement, I am not alone.
My husband and I perfect our routines
and modify our confines to suit us.

My seasonal decorations have shifted
for the duration of the pandemic perhaps,
since the next change is Halloween.

I notice each miniature at different times,
focusing on their details and how they
became a part of my life. I love color and texture.

Many "experts" advise using candles,
flowers, get a pet to spark things up.
I use what I have now. Avoid going out.

My husband made a mask of a tee-shirt
sleeve and paper insert. People are so
clever with fabric and design.

Since I do not plan to go out for weeks
and have been home for weeks, no masks,
no gloves, just hand-washing.

I chose Danish "hygge", making home
comfortable over Finnish "pantsdrunk",
getting drunk in underwear.

My calendar is full of crossed out
meetings, appointments and events.
I am content writing, perusing screens.

My cloister may not be totally spiritual,
more mundane, but taking a deep breath
and praying is a response to the turbulence.

Living Vicariously

Normally, my husband Court and I
grocery shop separately–he, to healthy
First Alternative and Fred Meyer.

I zip around on a red scooter at Safeway,
plucking easy to prepare meals
and dark chocolate.

For the first time we called in
our order to Fred Meyer for pick up.
Our pick-up time was a week later.

First he rambled in uncrowded
First Alternative, filling little bags
with tiny pellets of organic fare.

Then Fred Meyer. They have six
pick up slots. When you arrive at
your time, you call in to tell them.

Only two cars there and few in
the parking lot. Court was masked
and gloved. The food carrier was not.

He did not need the boxes he brought,
as there were plenty of paper bags.
When he unloaded, after a shower

and clothes change, I watched the
unveiling and checked the grocery list.
Everything we ordered was there.

I miss my scooter, seeing people in
person, not on page or screen. Our
mutual groceries un-bag, separate.

How long until we shop normally?
When will I stop self-quarantine
with my own delivery man?

Masks

Now everyone is expected
to wear a mask when going out.
Many diverse fabrics are selected.
Don't spread viral germs about.
>> Whether intentions good or bad,
>> an effective mask should be clad.

To wear a mask when going out
can be a fashion statement.
Medical or with artistic clout,
masks can bring disease abatement.
>> Pretend it is Halloween.
>> Faces don't have to be seen.

Many diverse fabrics are selected:
vacuum bags, HEPA and coffee filters,
pillowcases, flannel pajamas–you're protected.
Scarves, bandanas, patches from quilters
>> 3-D printers put to use.
>> Make one at home–no excuse.

Don't spread viral germs about.
Even with masks- stay six feet apart.
Not far enough for need to shout.
Kissing, hugging, expressing your heart
>> can find other touching ways.
>> You might need to find new pathways.

Whether intentions good or bad–
bank robber, medical worker, cashier,
delivery worker- some can mask a cad.
Masks create a suspicious atmosphere.
>> Will a burka or veil do?
>> A space helmet protect a few?

An effective mask should be clad
during this contagious time.
When face-freedom returns we'll be glad
we can gather in groups and it's not a crime.
>> Masks cover mouths, expose the eyes.
>> What are we hiding? Can we disguise?

People Fasting

*By immersion into nature in solitude, we allow the natural human to be
entrained to the nature of the planet...camping in solitude in nature...I jokingly
call it my People Fast.* Stephanie Nash

During this shelter-in-place,
social distancing time, we
avoid close contact with
people. A few are camping.

We are people fasting in
homes or the homeless
on the streets, temporary
shelters. Some in solitude.

It is a time to reflect, refresh,
re-group, re-ground, re-create.
Some have yards and gardens
to share our solitude moments.

We need to adapt to our confines,
contemplate how to handle
uncertainty. People appear
on screens, not at our door.

If we have errands, we wear
masks and gloves. We create
our breathing bubble and don't
cough germs on others.

I prefer the comfort of my home
to camping for my People Fast.
When I go into my backyard,
inhale chi without a mask, I escape

the inside filtered air, the protective
walls keeping others out. But I
do not forget those who cannot
people fast and breathe safely.

All's Quiet on This Western Front

When I go into the backyard, my husband's
husbandry includes digging compost and
shoveling it into a side pile, silently.

He is at the western part of the yard,
away from my garden focus on the other
side of the yard. I can't blame him

for the absence of birds, and the fireworks
were over last night. I'm sitting in my usual
spot which the birds ignored before.

After the mowing three dandelions
(2 in garden) and three buttercups remain.
The neighbor's dog does not bark.

Only white butterflies today, nicely spaced,
engaging flights. But no birdsong. Calm
before the storm? I must not read meaning

into patterns I cannot decipher. I am nervous
about eye surgery tomorrow, but today
I bake in warm, mid-afternoon sun.

Finally a jay emerges from the rhododendron,
walks through wire fence to our neighbor's
and belly flops, spreads wings—not out of sight.

Another jay goes over, beak to beak they greet.
They return. One belly flops in our garden spot,
then they scuttle under azaleas to their rhodie home.

My husband plucks raspberries and blueberries
from the branches. The wind chimes barely ting.
The pinwheel limply spins. All is calm, quiet.

Well, I came out to see a show, not a pantomime. I'd
like a little noise, a few showy moves. Not today. I leave
my pillow on the chair, hope for more action tomorrow.

Scheduling Our Day in Shut Down

During
shut down we can't
go to meetings, most stores,
appointments, gatherings unless
we're masked.

We stay
inside, wash hands,
decide what to do with
unscheduled time and when.
Puzzled.

Each day
face same challenge.
Certain tasks must get done.
But with the freed time, what should we
do first?

Each day
I can choose what
my focus should be and why.
What is necessary to be done
right now?

Each day
I dig deeper
inside my heart and soul.
Usually I'm too busy,
tired.

Each day
uncertainty,
how to cope with unknown.
Asking questions, receiving no
answers.

Scheduling During Pandemic

Daily
appointments axed,
events, classes cancelled,
calendar clears. I plan my day,
freely.

When I
eat or get dressed
is my choice. Where to go?
Many places closed, so no choice
to make.

Each day
what will I do?
What are priorities?
Self-quarantined also social
distanced.

In place
uncertainty
breeds creativity.
Responsibilities
still lurk.

Relax
in world out of
control? We're all in this
together? Inequities still
revealed.

From the Moon Room

Rain patters on the roof as I walk
into the Moon Room in my red cape,
about to observe the backyard.

For the first time I carry binoculars
to clarify some mysteries, but it
is too wet to go outside.

No wind to spin the pinwheel,
turn the weathervane, ring wind-chimes,
wave leaves or sway my metal angel,

rusty Airlika, who hangs from the apex
of the hazelnut branch arch over my chi
chair back, which drapes a raindrop necklace.

No shadows. No leaf-shine. No butterflies.
No birds, but I hear a chirping chorus
in the distance. No apple petal drops.

So I sit in an office chair at the center
table facing a black, red and gold ceramic
owl surrounded by Christmas decorations.

I know it is April. just some more quarantine
companions not put away in the Moon Room.
The Moon Room is an indoor-outdoor room.

A wall of windows faces the backyard. It
is like an enclosed porch with a green slate
floor and vaulted roof off the living room.

I pick up the binoculars and focus on
the backyard–up close–closer than when
I am contemplating and gathering chi there.

No creatures lurking in the canopies or
bushes or between fence slats. I return to
the Moon Room with sun symbols on its walls.

I'm in a miniature world of collections
of Lucias and Star Boys, wintery Annalee
felt figures, creches, decorated small trees,

a wall hanging with wooden angels,
Swedish folk art, a miniature village,
a clothes rack filled with ornaments,

a spiral wooden tree hung from the ceiling,
designed by my husband and filled with
family-made, painted wooden ornaments.

Behind me the toy chest and cradle my
parents made, a cigar box blue dresser
and my mother's doll Cindy–fading.

A huge hutch holds children's toys,
and decorations. A telescope of grandson
James, who named the Moon Room.

When he was little he loved to see the moon
through peaked windows above the main roof.
Memories of family parties here. A mosaic.

I put down the binoculars. The Moon Room
comforts me from the news beyond this quiet,
colorful place, where I contemplate my inverted navel.

The Knockers

No woodpeckers poking at trunks.
No delusionary birds hitting clear
window pane reflection in vain.

No solicitors for a good cause
or product, trying to convince
me to buy something I don't want.

The Mormon Elders and Jehovah
Witnesses wanting to save my soul,
can't even go to church, can't stop by.

No writers and Scrabble players
announcing their arrival–ready
share their flare for words.

No friends or family can visit,
walk through the door, catch up
and tighten bonds.

Less gavels dropping, for fewer
gatherings. Knocking for attention,
knock down other's intentions.

Knockers are on hold in their niches.
No head bangers in sight. We wait
to knock for new opportunities.

Chaos for Change

When you experience chaos, change is here... Chaos shakes up stuck energy and causes it to flow. When you notice things are falling apart and falling away, trust you are becoming unstuck. Sara Wiseman

Sitting comfortably at my computer
in my Corona cage, I am aware of chaos
globally and the inequities everywhere.

Trump followers twaddle his taradiddles
to open the shut down before chaos
is reined, endanger others, protesters or not.

Navajos without running water cannot
wash their hands. Food delivery hampered.
Health care inadequate.

On-line student education is mute if
your family does not have internet
equipment and you need school lunches.

Homeless do not have a place to
shelter in place. Unemployment causes
food lines, economic uncertainty.

We are stuck in place, when we need
to release our stuck-in-ness? The changes
are uncertain, unforeseen, unpredictable.

But then, what is our mission on this
unfathomable planet? Who sets the rules
and lets loose this chaos?

Earth leadership is inadequate, many
are ill-equipped for the challenges.
Chaos may have unstuck a toxic flow.

Masks For All Occasions

During this shut-down,
walls mask us from outside.
Illusion masks what's inside.

When I am able to emerge
from my COVID cocoon,
I have two types of masks.

One came from a grandson
in New Zealand, from China
distributed from California.

It is a white, medical-type mask,
like a bandage to promote
protection or healing.

The other came from a friend,
two-sided with colorful fabrics,
opens like an accordion.

It is a fashion statement. What
if we coordinated masks with
outfits? Are burkas good masks?

Apparently for extra protection
you can add nylon stockings.
At last, some way to wear them!

Masks can conceal bad intentions.
They have had a bad rap. Maybe
now they can serve a higher purpose?

Porcupine Hair

During the pandemic, I planned
to let my hair grow, to re-wild.
But it pokes out like a porcupine.

It's at an untamed stage. Combing
does little to make it conform to
any semblance of domestication.

Bangs dangle before my eyes,
constantly whisked away with
my wind-shield wiper hand.

My thin, straight locks even
managed a little curl by my ear,
a spring bouncing from my head.

I sleep and wake as if hair attacked
by a hurricane, not just wind-rumpled
but tornado twirled. Unruly chaos.

My spidery thin wisps are easily
misguided — a white fuzz-ball
like a blanched puffball.

If I try to cut it, I might inflict
bloody damage. So I'll go with
the flow, until I'm uncaged as it is.

Roaming in Place

Barefoot and in my nightgown,
I check my computer connections
to the shut down, wider world.

I have semi-scheduled my day.
Perhaps dressing should be
a priority. My feet are cold.

My interrupted sleep wakes
me from strange dreams.
Tidbits survive waking.

I constructed a shiny, papier-mache
alligator with uncontrollable controls,
sharp teeth and nasty temperament.

I was in a science fair and saw several
less lethal devices, when mine went
berserk. Did I pull the plug before waking?

Was it some lesson for this life or
a soul-splinter life in another dimension?
I never see what I look like as an observer.

In this 3D reality trying to move to 5D,
are dreams 4D or some other transition?
Do we ever really have a home, know origin?

Sheltering in this place, my thoughts
and dreams travel freely. No masks,
no social-distancing. True mobility.

A Saturday Ride

We decided to combine a list of errands
with a drive to the neighboring town of Philomath.
Our county opened up–somewhat—with restrictions.

Some restaurants had masked customers
inside. Others remained pick-up curbside.
Drive-thru lanes were busy.

We are only in phase one, so masks still
should be worn in public. Some are very
colorfully designed which might enhance face.

Apparently trikinis will be matching masks
with bikinis–but a bit early for this. Still
we can coordinate outfits and masks.

He was looking for solar panels. I was
looking at doors, color combos for houses,
irises, azaleas and rhododendrons.

When you are cooped up inside, you tend
to pay attention to details you may have
taken for granted and not noticed.

We discovered new neighborhoods we
never knew about with extraordinary
views of mountains and valley.

In our town, Saturday Market still took up
parking spots and stores needed to put up
signs so they did not take pick up spots.

Most marketers wore masks, but social
distancing not possible in that mob. We
did not shop. People bundled big bags.

We have been in shut down over two months.
Only the last three Saturdays have we gone
for a drive. We've entered few stores.

Though certain businesses are opening
with precautions, I am waiting awhile.
I have my masks handy, but in no rush.

Beyond Our Yard

On our second drive in so many
months beyond our yard at noon,
the sky is overcast, ground wet.

We have masks if we should stop
as we head down a main street
with long fast food lines.

We drive on streets with many flowering
azaleas, rhododendrons, a flat flower
that looks like sunny-side up eggs

On the campus, with no one in sight,
except one mask-less man who waves,
huge clusters of blooms reach to second story.

Then to the park where a crow pecks
road kill near few picnickers under shelters
who are not social distancing.

In Philomath the DQ gives me the wrong
drink, not diet and with ice. I don't drink it. But
the hot dog and chocolate dilly bar taste good.

In hilly neighborhoods in Corvallis, wild
turkeys infest yards and one yard has a
deer nibbling the leaves off a tree.

We stop at McDonalds to get me an
unsweetened iced tea. Long line into street.
They totally ignore his order. Tea is fine.

At home I sit behind windows to look at
our backyard. A jay flies onto a hazelnut
branch. Dandelions out of sight.

A brief sun casts shadows, highlights
the brilliant rhododendrons, azaleas
and allium in full bloom. Wind chimes ring.

A siren blares. I withdraw from the panes.
Our familiar backyard soothes. Beyond our
yard things appear normal— on the surface.

Pandemic Poets

Be well, do good work, and keep in touch. May Swenson

All shut in like Emily Dickinson or Hazel Hall,
poets venture out cautiously, have window view.
Poets face a new reality and protocol.
There is much confusion as to what to do.
　　　Inside and outside we seek clarity.
　　　Surrounded by lies and charity.

Poets venture out cautiously, have window view.
Like Emily and Hazel, our circumference limited.
We rely on screens for our flattened purview.
Masks required, gatherings not permitted.
　　　A time for mindfulness and reflection.
　　　A time for questioning and detection.

Poets face a new reality and protocol.
Events cancelled. Few places we can go.
Some not allowed to go out much at all.
Rapid change from just months ago.
　　　Consumed by uncertainty and fear,
　　　we wait puzzled until conditions clear.

There is much confusion as to what to do.
Conflicting suggestions and revelations,
for us continuously to review.
We cope with rescheduled staycations.
　　　Many work on poems in isolation.
　　　On-line contacts some consolation.

Inside and outside we seek clarity.
So much to muse on and sort.
Will we emerge with more parity?
What kind of insights will we report?
　　　What dark thoughts will we submerge,
　　　as we hope for light-filled lines to emerge?

Surrounded by lies and charity,
fake news and kindness side by side.
Will it lead to depression or prosperity?
Being in this all together, will we heal the divide?
　　　Poets can enlighten and heal.
　　　Pandemic poets can open and reveal.

Put on Our Masks

During the pandemic, I have not gone
into a building not medically required.
I wear a colorful mask. Duty done.
These visits under conditions not desired
       make me aware of the suffering around,
       why taking precautions is sound.

Into a building not medically required
without a mask is a future goal.
Now I wait for when shutdown's expired
and I can play a more normal role.
       Now I stay home most of the time
       not exposed to germs and grime.

I wear a colorful mask. Duty done
when I went to a doctor appointment not cancelled.
The return to normalcy has not begun.
My calendar has many cross-outs penciled.
       Not too many places I can safely go.
       How long this will be, I don't know.

These visits under conditions not desired
include have a temperature taken.
How many COVID results have been acquired?
How many tests are mistaken?
       When without symptoms, we are still contagious.
       Our pandemic leadership has been outrageous.

Make me aware of the suffering around
and help me be part of the solution.
May caring, kindness, healing abound.
May we have an equitable revolution.
       This helplessness is very wearying.
       A heavy load this planet is carrying.

Why taking precautions is sound,
is evident except for our pumpkin head leader.
He won't wear masks. Critics pound
questions and find him a fake news seeder.
       Each of us can wear a mask.
       That is not much to ask.

Visiting the Clinic

We approach the entrance
and see a short line, standing
six feet apart, waiting.
There is roof for a short line.

The line moves quickly.
They take your temperature
and write it down on a small
piece of paper. Not sure

what to do with it, so I stuff
it in a pocket. We are asked
if we are coughing. Everyone
is masked and socially observant.

At the elevator, each group
goes in, no mixing. You can't
bring children or friends to appointments,
only a medical care giver or for mobility.

The next line to tell them you are
there, also spaces out appropriately.
When the check-in clerk is ready for you
you move forward, confirm appointment.

Then you sit–away from everyone else,
observe the variety of face masks.
Some are very colorful like mine is. Then
wait for the nurse or tech to take you in.

My B-12 shot is ready. I bare my arm.
I have a short tee shirt on under my
hoodie. We are free to leave. But
at the exit–a downpour, torrential.

We decide I will wait undercover while
he dashes to get the car. He gets soaked.
But he would be more soaked trying to get
the wheelchair in the trunk as well in rain.

We decide to get comfort food en route
on our return to quarantine. A trip to the clinic
despite its bland, shiny, squeaky clean appearance
can hold unseen dangers, masked germy strangers.

Pandemic Patterns.

Stay home, social distancing,
washing hands often
enhancing

chances to stay safe and be well
not COVID 19.
Symptoms tell

if you are infected, but
sometimes no symptoms—
scuttlebutt.

In dangerous times,
death toll climbs

During Quarantine

Going into the third month of quarantine,
staying home, social distancing, masking,
washing hands, re-scheduling days.

Unclipped bangs grow below eyebrows,
need to be brushed aside. No dressing
up required– sweats, hoodies, jeans.

More time to write. More screen time
at computer and before TV. Sharp
phone is still pretty dumb with me.

As the weather improves I can sit
outside more and gather chi. My
husband takes daily bike rides.

We pick up groceries mostly by
ordering ahead and they are delivered
to the car. Sometimes quick stops in store.

I've only gone out to the clinic for
appointments and I am masked.
When we take a Saturday drive,

some people obey COVID-19 rules.
Others appear clueless, endanger others.
Children home-schooled. Some parents

unemployed, food distribution increased.
Businesses just beginning to reopen beyond
those deemed essential. I'll wait awhile.

We have ordered masks and a few other items
on line, but mostly use what we have and recycle.
In many ways life at home is much the same.

But meetings, events, face to face communication
postponed. Our new lighting will be just for us
–not family, friends, guests, writers, Scrabblers.

My quarantine companion and I are in the target
group for the virus. So far we are lucky, safe,
comfortable, hopeful amid the maelstrom.

Dandelion Dilemma

In a world full of roses,
stand out like a dandelion
in the middle of the lawn.

June Stoyer

Eftsoons
	soon after. Word of the day.

Eftsoons mowing the backgarth,
lawn monotones green without
light spots of white and yellow.

I gaze at the pops of color before
the methodical mower decapitates
heads he deems weeds.

Six yellow dandelions line the rock wall.
One puffball mid-yard awaits wind.
A metropolis of buttercups to the east.

Some suburbs near apple tree and
compost pile. Soon depopulated. We
are checking their names with friend.

The mower took a photo to send to her
to see if they are indeed buttercups or
some other flowers called weeds.

An obituary should at least have
the entity's name right for the mourners.
Perhaps each buttercup has a name?

Eftsoons the mowing under overcast
skies, I will not look at the massacre.
I'll hope tomorrow to see survivors.

During this pandemic we look for bright
spots to uplift morale. Deaths of any kind
bring sorrow eftsoons.

Yellow Sparks

The backyard drips rain. Tootsie,
the immovable weathervane
angel, stolidly gets drenched.

Airlika, the rusty angel is missing
from her hazelnut limb to get
a protective layer from further rust.

The pinwheel can get a wind-dry
if a good gust spins it. But wind
chimes are silent, so not windy.

My black metal chair wears a necklace
of translucent gems on its shoulders,
fringe from the arms, drops from sieve seat.

Rain dribbles off the roof and leaves.
The hose and watering can are
gone from the soaked garden.

Through the streaked window,
I strain to see if any buttercups
or dandelions survived recent mowing.

These yellow sparks warm my spirit.
There they are—in a dip in the lawn,
and sparsely sprinkled in the soggy grass!

They shine as if earth stars ready to join
the cosmos? Or star-drops from the sky,
maybe crying over the mower's decapitations?

Yellow sparks brighten their surroundings.
Sunny spots for the soul. Somehow during
this dark time, they have become important.

I have noticed them more this spring. I
mourn their passing. When their uplifting
season ends, our sad season will not.

What will replace these yellow spots? Will
mottled, fallen leaves elicit such joy? Alas,
life is transitory. Yellow sparks ignite my heart.

Control Freaks

Restless wind reins neighing,
braying branches. I nest indoors.
Windows shield me.

Earlier, rain gully washed the car.
It is a week and one day since
the mangling mower clipped the yard.

He grabs his Fisker hand mower
and methodically slaughters the lawn.
He's proud of his organic, quiet technique.

While he's in the front yard, I look
at the backyard with buttercup profusions
and stalwart dandelion near the rock wall.

He claims the wind has dried the grass
enough to mow. The captive pinwheel can't
spin on its own volition. Yard angels watch.

Safe garden plants, weeded to his
preferences, can witness what they
escaped. Too late for compost pile.

Only gardens can have color? Lawns
must conform to green? Control freaks
confine many aspects earthly life.

Perhaps the absent-minded professor
will run over a mislaid tool, kibosh
his intentions, permit a reprieve?

Soon he will finish the front yard and
begin his attack on the backyard. I do
not want to look at a battlefield cemetery.

I flee my nest, return to my computer,
where I can control what I see, if not
what there is to see.

The Dandelion Destroyer's Response

You see my push reel mower is more reliable and quieter. I stealthfully decapitate dandelions. They feel no pain and go to feeding the health of the yard.
Court Smith

It is slander to call dandelions "weeds"
and justify decapitation for your needs.
"Don't cut my time short," a dandelion pleads.

Why do you consider it your duty
to sacrifice such glowing beauty
when they are such a lawn cutie?

Your method of mowing does not matter
whether less painful or quieter, dandelions scatter
in bits to feed, nourish grass... yellow batter.

I want them to survive as flowers,
treated with respect–sun showers.
Not a weed, which bends and cowers.

Stand tall puffballs, puff seeds away.
Mowers grind seed in grass, prey
on towheads in shining array

Grass is not entitled to all of the lawn.
Dandelions are not just a pawn.
Unwatered this summer, grass is gone.

Methodically Mowing

Earlier our methodical mower
mowed the backyard east to west,
leaving my chi chair on the patio.

He carries the chair to a sunny spot
near the hazelnut tree. I follow with
my blue pillow to soften my seat.

A decapitated dandelion flays on
a patio stone. The five dandelions
lined near my office wall are now two.

The uniform boring yawn of a lawn
variegates with shadows, which start
and stop like neighbor's power mower.

He mumbles and grumbles as he mows
east to west, talking to himself in an angry
tone, as the mower quits and restarts.

Each time the drone stops, I am hopeful
he's done. Birdsong and wind-chimes
can't drown out the moaning mowers.

I wait, over-double my daily dose of
recommended nature time. I want
peace and quiet to grieve for lawn.

Three white butterflies grace the garden.
They are a symbol of artist Milan Rai, from
Nepal to invite global change and interaction.

Sparrows and hummingbirds check out
the blueberry bushes. Jays grasp power lines
when they could have mossy branch landings.

One jay flits pear tree, to blueberry bush to
apple limb where his cushioned landing pad
provides some nibbles before another takeoff.

When the methodical mower next door finally
puts his mower in the shed, the sun warms
my back. Bird chirps waft overhead.

As I return inside, I pick up the dandelion
head and gently place it by a survivor. One
of the many losses I can't prevent and mourn.

The Monotone Manscaper

The Wily Whacker attacked
the backyard this morning to
mow a monotonous green lawn.

It was after five before I could
face the massacre of color in the yard,
the southeast-northwest mowing stripes.

Going green in this case is over-kill.
He changes his three mowing patterns,
but he remains a manipulative manscaper.

Since there are no shadows, limpid
sun to warm me, I leave my chi-gathering
chair on the stone pavers of the patio.

A friend suggests the red azaleas
and rhododendrons lining the fence
are a color-compensation for dandelions.

To her the red brings solace. To me
my bleeding heart. To my delight–three
yellow dandelions and eight puffballs!

I see a mid-sized white butterfly
and two stellar jays peer down from
the power pole. No wind for chimes.

My yard angels are tranquil, looking
west, horns ready to toot whenever
sound infiltrates their being,

A delicate puffball seed wafts before me.
I watch its flight, then it lands on the patio
beside me. Hope a wind-gust carries it further.

My glasses are being corrected with a new
lens. I squint my cataract-filled eye and perceive
through my cataract-free eye this situation.

Intuitive friends assure this shut down will
lead to a changed, light-filled world. As color
returns with spring, nature eludes manscapers?

Manscape Redefined

The term manscape sounded like a perfect
word for people's impact on the landscape.
I tend to focus on over-zealous mowers.

The first manscape definition is to manage
a man's body hair with waxing and other
cosmetic products (especially below the waist).

Lawn Mower 3.0 is the best groin trimmer,
safe in a shower and to groom your "twigs
and berries." I looked at a second definition.

Rare: to impose shape on a landscape
to suit humans. Then a landscape that
has been shaped by the human race.

Aha! finally the context I want for my
pro-dandelion campaign. But what about
the other, ahem, intimate connotations?

Well, I like manscape as an intervention
to remove excess landscaping growth.
It places responsibility for dastardly deeds.

Manscapers want to control how
natural growth should be pruned,
no matter where "weeds" appear.

Manscaper has a too masculine bent.
Humanscaper doesn't quite cut it.
Back to steward, gardener?

I'm just too much of a feminist
to use manscaper any more. I prefer
people to steward and garden.

But I can insert negative adjectives
in front of mower if I want and I will.
Dandelion Power! Dandelion strong!

My Dandelion Patch

The day after Earth Day is sunny.
The Morbid Mower announces, he
is chopping off the heads of dandelions.

He mows the front yard first, giving
me time to mourn the backyard. I go
to the window to bid the lawn farewell.

I can't watch the slaughter. He assures
dandelions are indestructible and will
come back. But later when I go outside,

the yard will be a hacked, dead zone.
How can I gather chi amid dandelion
carcasses? Should I give them healing time?

I hope many crouch to pop up when
he leaves, all smug and macho mower.
Dandelions, bow before the mower and live!

Earth Day gatherings were canceled
do to social distancing and shut down
guidelines. Protesters infect each other.

But they were protesting not for the Earth
but for selfish reasons and from ignorance.
My backyard patch is part of Earth's quilt.

Dandelions design my patch with sunny
glow in dark times. They are survivors
and patch places in need of light.

After Mowing

Reluctantly I venture into the butchered
backyard to contemplate and loop chi.
Grass blades bent or broken.

One defiant puffball straightens
and continues procreating. One
dandelion peeks from crushed lawn.

The lawn itself is a mishmash
of ground covers as if squished
and mashed by a tornado.

A tiny bird (who might be a hummingbird)
flitters amid the blueberry bush. A stellar
jay primps and flutters on the pear branch.

Overall a docile scene. The wind-chimes
whimper. Neighbor's power mower mutes.
My inner turbulence exhales in deep breaths.

A momentary pause from confinement,
but a hacked yard is not comforting. Beauty
appears in red azalea flares near the fence.

I prefer taming my mind than nature.
A loyal, white butterfly appears as usual,
a mourning dove coos nearby.

While Dandelions Smile

Today is mowing day.
We are on an eight-day cycle
from a former twelve-day cycle.

Dandelions have fewer days
to shine and replenish. Can
I face another beheading?

He says he will postpone
mowing until after I go outside
to commune with nature.

But tomorrow the dastardly deed
will be done. I have to be
Dandelion Strong.

Inside or outside I witness peril.
News is grim, but they have good
news segments–light sparks.

I peer out the window at my bright
spots–yellow dots of mirrored shine.
How long is their season?

How long is the shut down? Yesterday
I spied a small yellow plastic disc in the lawn.
Probably a toy tossed to a child or dog.

Perhaps he will not see it and it gives
his mower blades a tussle. Grass blades
will sway freely, while dandelions smile.

Dazzled by Dandelions

The Saturday before Easter
is 65 and sunny. I rush to
the backyard door to go outside.

A dazzling array of dandelions—
at least doubled since yesterday—
lures me into their midst.

In my eagerness to escape my
Corona cage, I forgot to pick up
my blue pillow for my chi chair.

I sit on hard black metal, more
like reality beyond these confines,
even seen through sunglasses.

In all directions the dandelions shine.
The tall puffball blew its wad overnight.
Four puffballs had a growth spurt, but hold tight.

Apple and Pear blossoms expand.
Small brown birds prance among
the blueberry mini-buds.

White butterflies put on an aerial show
the likes I've never seen. From West and East
they take a respite from zig-zag flight and fly away.

Usually I see one. I attribute them as message
carriers from deceased beloveds, but today?
They still must allow mass gatherings in heaven.

Two butterflies met mid-yard, circled each
other in a dance, then flew off in different
directions. I wonder who they were?

Dew-diamonds flash in grass and in rock wall
crevice in a spider web. A gentle jangle of
wind-chimes. A pinwheel spin. Angels still.

I am grateful I have this spot of nature, a home
to shelter in, a stockpile of supplies. But I am aware
of the inequities outside the confines of my experience.

No lofty thoughts among these wings.
I am earthbound like the dandelions.
But I'm interconnected with everything.

When I peer above the sunglasses' rim,
the world looks brighter. But a sun-glassed
world somehow is more soothing.

I nod farewell to the dandelion behind my chair,
I look back at my pre-Easter resurrections.
Tomorrow could it be even better?

Aftermath

In an effort to appease me from the effects
of his mowing mania, he graciously puts my
chi chair back on the lawn out of shadows.

He jumps on the metal seat to entrench its
place in the green decor until the next
dandelion massacre. I bring my blue pillow.

It is Unicorn Day–as much of a fantasy
as my dreams for a dandelion oasis.
Fantasy escapes are needed in current reality.

My only outdoor excursions for weeks have been
going into the backyard when it is sunny to breathe
unfiltered air, revive in nature and sun-spots.

Two dandelions escaped to the garden. Four
hunkered below the mower. I am delighted.
They are my focus, not the clipped lawn.

I do notice the pink buds on the apple and hazelnut
trees, white blooms on strawberry plants and pear
limbs. But yellow rays of dandelions are my favorites.

We do not know how long the pandemic will last,
how long we will social distance, face shut-downs,
overly washed chapped hands, when we can touch.

Soon dandelion season will be gone. Will azaleas
irises and rhododendron beauty console me?
I must remember how to cope without dandelions.

Still there are sunflowers. I am so glad most flowers
are in the un-mowed garden. The wily weeder can
pick on weeds more people agree are weeds.

The Lawn Lecture

Emeritus Professor and Master Mower strolls
into the backyard where I am inhaling chi,
to report yellow pollen on our car windshield.

Then he proceeds to lecture on Lawn Diversity
and the Threat Dandelions Present. He pulls
tall grasses from the wall and base of tree trunks.

He declares we grow Kentucky Bluegrass, fescue,
clover, native grasses and several other varieties in
our lawn. He does not want them crowded out by dandelions.

He points out the leafy patches dandelions leave.
Looks like the clover and other grasses have room.
Some blades bowed before the mower and survived.

In the absent-minded professor way he steps
on two puffballs enhancing their journey to seed.
He avoids the four fully arrayed yellow flowers.

He knows I am a dandelion devotee and I ignore
his pontifications when I choose. A bee lands
on a hazelnut branch above me. Ants underfoot.

A stellar jay rests on a barren garden spot. Loyal
white butterfly puts in an appearance. They all love
dandelions and are on my side. Shadows sketch.

He composts his fist-full of grasses and goes
inside. The sun warms my back. I loop chi from
Earth to cosmos. The dandelions wink at me.

Slaughtering Shine
        Mowing the lawn on Passover.

Before Macho-Hand-Mower-Fiskar Man
returns from his bike ride to mow the lawn,
I methodically blow seven puffballs into the grass.

The dandelions seeds float and nestle,
while dandelions in full array, display
their spot of sunshine, face slaughter.

I could not risk he would pull the puffballs
and throw them on compost. I hope low-
lying dandelions escape the mower.

I asked him to postpone mowing until
after Easter so I could enjoy the dandelions
on these few sunny days while I sit outside.

After days of rain, peering outside windows
in quarantine, being cooped up and
a distant observer for days, I crave sun rays.

In my haste to blow the seeds, I forgot
to put the pillow on my chi chair under
the hazelnut tree. I sit on hard black metal.

My dandelion companion near my foot
has mysteriously disappeared. I notice
a cluster of three-leafed clover nearby.

A white butterfly scribbles condolences.
Angels and pinwheel are still. Birds chirp.
Wind-chimes knell dolefully. But dandelions shine.

He's in the front lawn butch-cutting the grass,
a reminder of his college haircut and youth?
I'll head inside for an overdose of dark chocolate.

Shadows encroach my lair, foreshadowing
darkness. My chi chair's legs are dug in deep.
Better he has to tug them out, rather than dandelions.

These days we are thanking helpers for their
service. I whisper thanks for the towheads'
beauty and shine. May they resurrect by Easter.

A Dandelion Day

Sun streams through the windows.
I gaze at the backyard straining
to see the dandelions mirror the sun.

I am eager to get dressed and sit
amid spring's blossoms and blades.
When confined inside, they bring joy.

My husband gives me his bike ride report.
Many walkers, probably as many as cars.
Walkers with dogs and children. Few bikers.

All ages gardening in their yards
enjoying the sunny, dandelion day.
I will be our backyard's observer.

Midday, as shadows straight-forward north,
I pull up my blue hoodie to protect from
the overhead sun and venture forth.

My chi chair is in roof shadow. My husband
pulls the legs from mushy soil when he mows.
He says it aerates the soil. I can't move it.

He tugs the chair free, moves it, jumps on
the seat to stomp it firmly into the lawn. I put
my pillow down. A dandelion glows at my side.

Dew sparkles on grass blades like the diamond
on my hand. Above me pink buds emerge
from the crusty apple and hazelnut trees.

Since yesterday the dandelions formed new
configurations. Puffballs poofed, seeds
sprouted. New puffballs await the wind.

The pinwheel spins spasmodically. But
these puffballs are not ready to blow.
Wind-chimes chime encouragement.

I am content to see their gray, seedy heads—
mini-clouds. I am alone communing with
nature. These walls and fences don't feel

confining. More guardians and protectors.
I suppose our house walls do the same
as we await the pandemic to pass.

Amid dandelions I sit in the sun, breathing
chi, warming my body and soul. I am
out of shadows' reach for a little while.

When I pick up the blue pillow, his chocolate-
milky, muddy footprint dries on the chair. My
dandelion chums shine under blue skies.

A Dandelion Miracle

Under an overcast chilly sky,
mid-Monday afternoon after Palm
Sunday, National Dandelion Day,

and Queen Elizabeth's keep a stiff
upper lip speech, I carry my blue pillow
into the backyard to sit in my chi chair.

On my husband's morning trowel prowl,
he found the pillow had a sleep-over
on my chi chair and he drier-puffed it.

Hugging the pillow to my chest, to my
delight the dandelions had doubled
overnight and five were puffballs!

No shadow. No wind. Few birds.
But dandelions polka-dotted sun
on the unmown lawn. I about cried.

Overhead the apple and hazelnut
canopies sprouted tiny leaflets. Metal
angels' horns muted. Wind-chimes stilled.

With no accompaniment or fanfare,
softly I sang the chorus of Hallelujah
to the burgeoning dandelions.

Prime Minister of New Zealand declared
the tooth fairy and Easter bunny as
"essential workers". Next Sunday, chocolate

Cadbury eggs perhaps, even if Easter
gatherings and making baskets postponed?
By then more dandelions will resurrect.

As I carry the pillow inside, a deep wind
chime knells. I will tell our mower not to
mow the backyard at least until after Easter.

Uprooting

Mid-afternoon the shadows stretch east
across the backyard. I am dressed, wear
shoes. It has warmed enough for a jacket.

I push my pillow-carrying walker to my
bare chair and sit with a dandelion at my feet.
On National Dandelion Day I should join them.

A neighbor's motor mower drones. When it stops
a siren, car horn beeps, barking dogs, a plane.
Wind-chimes clang. Then the grim-reaper comes.

He props the leaning fence with wooden boards
then attacks and whacks holly, blackberry, poison oak,
grassy mounds in the bark dust. He frees boundaries.

He clears stones separating garden and lawn.
He is about order and organization. Don't
infringe in another plant's place–he decrees.

He imposes his vision for the world on his
fifth acre. Tall grass whiskers on rock walls,
blade bristles in the chives–he shaves them.

He sees a weedy world. He leaves blueberry,
raspberry and strawberry plants alone. White
strawberry blooms smile beneath white pear flowers.

The poor barren peach had pink blossoms,
but not now. No leaves like the plum tree.
Apple and hazelnut trees are late-bloomers.

Birds from branches and power-lines chirp.
Are they chortling, chastising, sending greetings
to the bee-havens, bug umbrellas below?

I search for constellations of dandelions–
three trio clusters, puffball pair, two soloists.
Shade shifts from the dandelion at my feet.

The petals radiate, glow. Through side fence
slats a sparkling yellow glass ball sparkles
like a spotlight for the dandelion show.

A motor-mower grumbles again. I trust the
grim-reaper will respect dandelions today.
His uprooting might get poison oak revenge.

Celebrating With Dandelions

Sunday morning barefoot, wearing my nightgown,
I walk to the screened back door to wish
the very few dandelions Happy Dandelion's Day.

Shadows stretch west. Pinwheel spins, birds
chirp, wind-chimes jingle for dandelions,
chips of sun, under a breezy, blue sky.

I supposed the dull blades of grass are jealous
of the attention given to a brighter bunch. But
I prefer more colorful sorts, less uniformly glum.

Then I go to the front door. Several clusters
of dandelions filled gaps into radiant patches.
Grass is just a background fabric of yard quilt.

Few cars pass by and no pedestrians
to add to the chorus. But the clear, cloudless
sky will let them shine on their special day.

Later I might even attempt dressing and sit
in the backyard to slurp some chi. When it
is warmer I can greet them up close.

I do not even have to worry about social
distancing. I can gaze at their sun-glow
faces and be thankful they are beside me.

I don't want to hear mowers, see gardeners
plucking them from their places, pickers unless
they will eat them–not even a bouquet today.

A thing of beauty belongs everywhere, entitled
to their own bit of sun. I spy a frizzy, fuzzy puffball
and smile. It reminds me of un-manicured me.

In Defense of Dandelions

He returns from a bike ride, a brief
respite from quarantine, spritzed
by rain and hopefully no germs.

In another brief break from rain, he mowed
the lawn. This champion of diversity in
most things slaughtered dandelions.

He touts his organic yard, his multi-
variegated grasses, his carefully cared
for clippings–intolerant of "weeds".

How can such a kind, generous man
not appreciate the beauty, color and
texture of dandelions in his lawn?

As I gaze at a few garden survivors,
two hugging the wall- a puffball and bright
young'un, I see one mid-yard beacon.

I can envision my own twilight zone–not
standard, but a flourishing pond of yellow
dandelions suffocating the green grass.

Tuffs of yellow with some elderly gray
puffs to keep them proliferating. Yeah
gray! Yeah yellow! Yeah sun-mirror!

If he at least ate his dandelion crop,
in salad, tea or wine instead of just
chopping them to bits–maybe justified?

Naw, not going to happen. Dreams dim
in this nightmare reality. But when the curve
flattens, maybe I'll find some dandelion seeds.

Through a back fence gap, a light from
our neighbor shines a dandelion eye, a sparkle
of yellow toward our overly-green yard.

National Dandelion Day
    Sunday, April 5th, 2020

Tomorrow is National Dandelion Day.
I must prepare to honor the weed
and the flower, I have so often praised.

To a gardener it is a weed, unless
partaking of its edible and medicinal
properties like tea, wine, soup, salad.

To floral admirers they are a gift to
our eyes, a child's bouquet to mother,
color and texture enhancing the lawn.

Tomorrow thou shalt not mow, toss
dandelions into compost, treat them as
a nuisance weed. Just appreciate their beauty.

I am not a fan of dandelions as an edible
for I don't care for salads, teas or wine, many
soups. I'll get ABCD in other forms.

Tomorrow nourishing rain should fall
to add to dandelions' flourishing. Maybe
some wind for puffball gusto?

I will be especially vigilant our versatile
dandelions are not disturbed tomorrow,
but like today, I will gaze at them in adoration.

Dandelions: The Super FLower

The dandelion is one of the most generous and useful plants, yet many folks poison it. Go figure. Tribune News Service

We have an organic garth
for dandelions to grow,
but they are dug up and
clipped when we mow.

I love the yellow flowers,
our mower calls weeds.
He loves to decapitate them
for his misguided needs.

Dandelions are rich in vitamin A,
calcium, fiber, vitamin C,
iron and potassium—so eat them
or just let them be.

Flowers can make wine.
Dried roots can be a tea.
It has also been touted as
a detox remedy.

Leaves before flowering
or mature in the fall,
make raw and cooked
greens for us all.

So if you are committed
and change your lethal ways,
don't forage in weed killer places,
be vigilant for bees always.

Dandelions have toothy leaves
the flower stalk is leafless, hollow,
filled with a milky latex, it blooms
a beautiful, sunny yellow.

If one thinks of them as flowers
not weeds, not blemish but food,
they become a mood enhancer
and make your yard look good.

Dandelions nourish bees and us
but face floral discrimination.
Treat them as productive, with respect,
and protect-that's my loyal determination.

Maddening

On an overcast, chilly, breezy afternoon
I go to deep breathe and gather chi, to
seek solace from the turbulence in the world.

Sunday, our town had a peaceful protest of
4000 without police presence. I was feeling
optimistic the upheavals might bring change.

I sit down and survey the mowed, too green
lawn, devoid of yellow, flattened, clipped
and writhing blades. Two buttercups left.

I looked toward the towering dandelion garden
refugees for comfort. The methodical mower
pulled them out, when he knew I loved them.

Frantically, I look for survivors. Three in other
areas of the garden escaped. When he returns
from his bike ride, I will defend these spots of sun.

All the floral plants wither, fade. Stellar jays
rustle rhododendrons, hustle azaleas. One jay
clenches the wire fence and nibbles decaying buds.

The noisy motors of our neighbors whir and whine.
I am in no mood for them today. In the patio pavers,
a thin-leafed plant with tiny purple flowers surrounds

the base of the stalk holding a metal blue jay, like
a wreath. Others climb the house wall. I will add
them to the list of endangered species in our yard.

My anger has not lessened when he returns home.
I let him have it and let him know–no excuses and
no reason to deliberately hack garden and patio plants

under my protection. I concoct revenge should
he destroy joy in areas off limits. He kills enough
yellow blooms in the lawn with his mowing addiction.

Ah! to re-wild the yard. Back to the days when yards
grew crops and enjoyed free-flowering plants. Justice
for all living essences. Slow changes madden.

A Seven Dandelion Day

When I went into the backyard to gather
some chi, the dandelions had spread to seven.
My husband dug out the front yard dandelions.

Three in the garden are super-sized sun spots.
The lupin look spikier. Pink peach blossoms
blush from the top of the tree.

No clouds to mute the blue or sound of planes.
The roof-line shadow shades part of my chair,
which is stuck sturdily in the grass.

Airlika angel has unhinged at her head from
the hazelnut limb and dangles by her feet, a whirling
shadow amid the stolid tree trunk shadows.

Her head spouts the broken metal hook, like a flute
to accompany her tooting horn. Tootsie, the lazy
weathervane angel stubbornly points north.

Knotty, crusty trunks conceal buds.
Slow progress in the emergent grounded
color patches. No bugs. Few birds.

One jay perched on the power line, dropped
to the barren dirt. A second jay joined in
and they circled each other before flying off.

I hear chirps in the distance. Are they also
social distancing? A siren reminds not all is well.
Pinwheel, whirligigs, wind-chimes slow dance.

Sun sneaks through the metal mesh on the back
of my black chi chair. I take my deep chi breaths,
huff and chuff my chakras. My outdoor time's up.

As I am about to leave, a stellar jay lands on
the blueberry bush to bid me farewell. I am grateful
for this nourishing plot to heal and renew my spirit.

133

Chi-Gathering in Summer

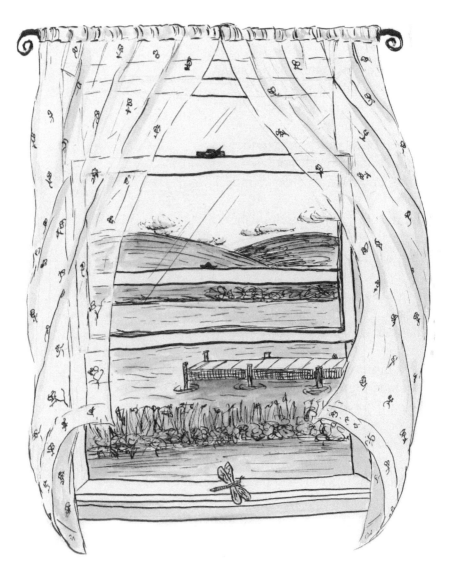

Stop looking at the walls,
look out the windows.

Katie Pilkington

Sun-gentling

The methodical mower mows
the top tier of the backyard.
I sit on the bottom and breathe deep,

not just to draw chi, but to contain
my anger at the clipped lawn.
Mown grass massages ground?

Unseen birds cheep in lavender
rhododendron. Red rhodies
wither and fade. Azaleas crimp.

Red rose buds on a small bush
far from lush irises and chives.
A squashed mushroom by my chair.

The canopy shadows sway a slow
dance on the smoothed dance floor.
The rock wall is the wallflower.

Eight buttercups cluster in lowland.
Six embedded in the pebbles between
the patio pavers. Maybe mower won't see.

Airlika angel has returned with her shiny
restorative layer over encrusted rust. She
hangs with hazelnut leaf patterns on her back.

Sun warms my back and soul. Mind stirs
like the lazy pinwheel. Wind chimes gently
rebuff siren, airplane and traffic noise.

For a brief respite it is about chi, living, not
uncertainty and death. Despite mowing. I'm
balancing better, depending on sun and beauty.

Casting Shade on the Backgarth

Not cloud nor contrail scars sky.
Warm, clear— a perfect day
to cast shade, dance shadows.

For several days there's been a darth
of winged-ones in the garth. This saddens
me, as I windshield wipe my gaze to view.

Within minutes a stellar jay darts
into the bedraggled red rhododendron.
Then another jay snacks in the garden.

A third jay nestles in apple branches.
The finale is two white butterflies which
criss-cross the yard, but don't land.

Other birds cast shadows as they fly above
my head, but the aerial show is over.
Windblown pinwheel's shadow flickers beneath.

Canopies' shadows waltz with
the wind. Wind chimes accompany.
My shadow lumps in my chi chair.

A red embroidered Andean hat
protects my pale face, my back
to the sun deters sunburn.

The garth's angels maintain their stance
Airlika shines and sways from a hazelnut
branch. Weathervane Tootsie is stagnant.

Shadows darken, cool this tranquil
place where all appears normal, while
I cast shade on this turbulent time.

Waiting it Out

After several chilly minutes
gathering chi in the backyard,
the overcast sky moves on.

Shadows sharpen and the sun
warms my thinly-covered back. My
Andean hat shades my pale face.

One white butterfly and one
Stellar jay make a flash-by. Two
sparrows perch on a peach limb.

These quarantine days, birds have
less noise and air pollution to deal
with. But now the cities are burning.

Curfews try to curb the violence.
Masks contend with smoke.
The atmosphere is heavy.

I'm cheered by two defiant dandelions
facing the rock wall, the resilient sprinkle
of buttercups, burgeoning mushrooms.

Here the air has cleared. The machine
sounds pause. The wind gives the pinwheel
a whirl and the wind chimes a jangle.

Airlika, the rusty angel hangs above me
on a hazelnut limb. Her coated face shines.
Tootsie, the weathervane angel, does not budge.

In this tranquil place can I calm my
raging thoughts? Can the black and white
images surrounded by flames burn out?

Our hose meanders through the garden
unused due to recent rain. Hosing nor pepper
spray has dampened the violent protests.

As if Covid-19 is not enough. As if
an incompetent president is not enough.
As if virulence everywhere is not enough.

Not everyone has a place to retreat to.
Not everyone gets an equitable shake.
Not everyone can choose what to do.

Watching Without Metaphor

On warm, sunny, just-summery mid-afternoon,
I carry my blue pillow to soften my chi chair,
seeking respite from my agitated soul.

I am not probing for omens, meaning,
metaphors for what I see, just a calming
presence to relieve my weariness.

I don't ask why there are no white butterflies,
why blue jays fly solo as shadows overhead
or spread-eagle in an open garden spot,

or why jays prefer the lush lavender rhododendron
to the languishing pink azalea– red from both
flowers leeched from their bloody prime,

or why the white irises continue to thrive
as well as purple chive or why no dandelions
survived the mowing, mushrooms smooshed,

or why one buttercup ducked mid-lawn, but
a buttercup cluster de-populated, no bees,
bugs or birdsong as much as usual,

or why gusts of wind salsa the canopy shadows
with gusto, the wind chimes clang arrhythmically,
leaves Tootsie, the angel weathervane, immobile.

The garth rises my curiosity, garners my focus
as the sun pelts my shoulders, my Andean
hat shades my face, but I still have qualms.

I leave the blue pillow on the chair. Deep breathe.
A glistening spider string straddles a hazelnut
branch to my chi-gathering chair. I don't break it.

Diverting Darkness in the Light

A Pleiades of buttercups sparkle
under the roof shadow, as I carry
my blue pillow to my chi chair.

I haven't even had a chance to sit
down, when a blue jay jettisons
across the backyard near me.

Today is a busy day for jays.
They even pair up to peck
beak to beak in the garden.

They fly to power lines and
the bedraggled peach tree,
grub beneath azaleas.

They belly flop in an open, flat
garden spot and spread their wings.
A power nap? A feather stretch?

But my attention diverts from wings,
when my husband brings the proof
of my book *Waves* from the publisher.

I have been impatiently waiting
to see it and check it out before
ordering some to give away.

I find a possible change and
decide to go inside to call Maureen
to see if it can be corrected easily.

But the jays have a grand finale for me.
One swishes by me as if closing the curtain.
Two circle each other in the open spot.

My warmed shoulders, back and heart
guide my overflowing walker away from
shadows and sun to contemplate changes.

Solar Healing

Mid-afternoon under a cloudless,
sky, I sit in the summer sun to warm
my sore neck, knees, shoulders, spirit.

I hat-cover to shade my face and my
clothes filter the sun's rays. Canopy
shadows blanket the grass.

A Stellar jay zooms to groom in
an open spot in the garden, belly flops,
spread-eagles, garners some sun.

I call this place a drop spot for so many
jays pause, flick feathers, twitch to itch
or scratch, laze in the sun, drop— what?

Another jay nose-dives past droopy,
irises, faded chives, ailing azaleas
to the debilitated rhododendron.

My thoughts drift to a dear friend
undergoing harsh treatments, the
people dealing with coronavirus,

the peaceful protesters pelted by
rubber bullets, pepper spray, pushed
by hard police shields. Violence. Fires.

A white butterfly circles the drop spot
and disappears. Bandage or surrender sign?
A blue jay manifests under a blueberry bush,

hops to the drop spot for a pause that
refreshes? Returns to the blueberry bush,
emerges to peck at the rock wall moss.

The jay looks right at me, proceeds to
the lawn, back to the drop spot. I do not
want to disturb the bird, so I wait to leave.

Finally, the jay disappears into the underbrush.
A "bluebird of happiness" omen? When the jay
hides, I haul my solar-powered hulk inside.

Momentary Visitors

The sun darkens and fades canopy shadows
amid clouds. As I sit in the backyard, gathering chi,
my back and shoulders never really warm.

Two dandelions goal post at opposite ends
of the yard. A caravan of buttercups manifest
destiny west. Most flowers brown, curl, drop.

Two white butterflies whisk by. The pinwheel
and wind chimes mostly still. Irises and chives
looking pretty shoddy. Apples bubble.

Two Stellar jays meet in the garden, flare feathers
and turn birdsong into bird-screech. A third bird
joins them and they quietly poke the garden.

One by one they fly in different directions. One
takes off from the ailing peach tree. Another
perches on top of Tootsie, the weathervane angel.

The launch causes her to swerve direction and
then she returns true north. The third jay leaves
from the wire fence. No more jays return.

Gray wind-drifter fluffs (probably from dandelions)
waft, then hide in the grass. Bugs buzz around me.
Swift and slow changes visit the garth.

When mechanical monsters begin to grind
and whine, I head inside, drop my blue pillow,
hope for more visitors to my home soon.

Searching for Meaning in the Garth

A near-summer, sunny afternoon
I head to the backyard to sort out
the chaos and deep breathe chi.

The irises de-petal, the dulled chives
turn gray, azaleas and rhododendrons
look rusty, but tiny red roses gush.

At least six white butterflies appear
to scribble messages in the air. At least
six Stellar jays flash and dash amid

the blueberry and rhododendron bushes.
They perch on a thin, weakened peach limb,
screech and chase each other to the next yard.

A neighbor greets me behind the fence,
interrupted by a mobile phone call
from my grandson. The other neighbor

talks baby talk to her dog. Bird and
canopy shadows wriggle in the breeze,
the wobbly pinwheel wind-whirls.

Intermittent music from the wind chimes.
Above me Airlika angel on the hazelnut
limb sparkles a spot of sun over her left eye.

Confusing signals from a puzzling world.
Any meaning to be found in my observations?
The sun warms my back and shoulders,

my hoodie protects my face. The blue pillow
on the metal chair feels lumpy. But no
mechanical sounds. Up vibes prevail.

I smile at the purple flowers still surrounding
the metal bluebird's stalk. Blooms push between
pavers. My walker ribs me as I go inside.

Blinking Shadows

Blinking
shadows under
canopies wink with sun.
Overcast skies erase shadows
quickly.

Angel
Airlika on
hazelnut limb shades her
belly, shine in her eye, gown
in shadow.

Backyard
shifts in breeze with
intermittent pinwheel,
spins, wind chimes, sky color, movements
shadowed.

Mushrooms,
buttercups hug
the ground, don't leak shadows.
They keep any light on top of
bloomings.

Constant
changes repeat
quicker when sun varies
intensity and direction for
shadows.

I watch
interplay of
light and dark, reflect on
current global issues, cheer
for sun.

Resonance in the Garth

When I went to deep breathe
to gather chi in the backyard,
I noticed species tend to cluster.

The mushrooms have divided
into two groups fairly near each
other. The older batch is darkening.

The chives stuck together and are
now clipped. The white irises had two
colonies– now all blooms vanished.

Rhododendrons and azalea bushes
alternate along the fence, look rusted.
Blueberry bushes and strawberry patch

claim their spot, become fruitful and
multiply. The tiny red rosebush is
all alone amid grassy weeds.

Buttercup brigade marches west,
picks up more recruits daily. Three
trailblazers reach mid-lawn.

The dandelions integrate the most.
Two tall ones guard a small blueberry
bush, one blown puffball amid clover.

Even one type of bird rustles among
the bushes. Stellar jays screech, but
rarely land to peck the garden dirt.

Two apple tree limbs interlace. Two
hazelnut trees embrace. Since they
are so close–they may interplay.

The solo pinwheel and the dual
wind chimes are at the will of the wind.
My two yard angels are not together.

The floral and arboreal species seem
more cohesive. Airlika, swaying on the
hazelnut limb sometimes gets sun- stroked.

Tootsie, the weathervane angel
stands firm against the wind–rarely
budges from her chosen direction.

It is overcast. Occasionally, the sun
breaks through and casts shadows.
I am pondering the strife of life.

How do you respond to systemic
injustice and disease? Despair?
Revenge? Redemption? Hope?

I researched Jewish and German
reactions to the holocaust. The
survivors had to face guilt, trauma.

Nazi leaders often chose suicide
and killed their children with them.
They feared retribution.

Concentration camp survivors were
often too weak to kill their guards,
but liberators killed many perpetrators.

Some Jews did become Avengers.
Generational German guilt remains.
Many did not have a choice how to respond.

How do we integrate diversity? How can
we respond when we seem unable to
control events? Protest? Vote responsibly?

In quarantine, we have plenty of time to
contemplate Black Lives Matter and needed
systemic changes behind our blunders.

Do I focus on the environment? Advocate
for progressive leadership and police reform?
My backyard plantings remain mostly segregated.

We are all in this together–flora and fauna.
I am old. Unfortunately the young carry a heavy
mantle. My moods fluctuate–glad, sad and mad.

Today is a cloudy day. Tomorrow is supposed
to be sunny. Do we change like the weather?
Switch directions with a karmic weathervane?

My Blue Pillow

My blue pillow, left from yesterday,
sun-warms my buns. My navy hoodie
protects my face. I'm a hunk of blue cheese.

Today is for fluttering fritillaries scribbling
lines across the garth. Two fly within
a foot of my head. Not a usual case.

About mid-sit a yellow butterfly with
black-edged wings crosses mid-yard—
a diverse beauty from blanched cousins.

Three Stellar jays perform their stints
emerging from a rhododendron curtain.
One by one they belly-flop and spread wings.

One flies to the back of Tootsie, the weathervane
angel. She stands firm, globally accepted,
unlike toppled Confederate statues.

Thirteen trailblazers continue the buttercup
quest west. Under the roof-line shadow
a cluster looks like stars in night sky.

When the weedy-greedy gardener comes
with his orange basket, I point out the beauty
of the buttercups, left from a delayed mowing.

He proceeds to behead the shriveled white iris
beside the decapitated chives. He pulls grass
whiskers from the forty-year old rock wall

he built from sidewalk chucks to create a tier
for the garden and open grassy area, We played
mini-golf with dug-in tin can holes there.

From my pillowed comfort, I am able to deep
breathe chi, spin chakras, calm and warm
the uncertainty and turbulence...for awhile.

As I was about to go inside, a white butterfly
flew right in front of me. I left the blue pillow
on my chi chair, believing in blue sky tomorrow.

White Butterflies

Today I saw an abundance of butterflies,
all but one white, probably garden whites
or cabbage whites. Maybe large moths?

I look for them and hope they appear.
Today two passed near my head and one
right in front of me. I could have touched them.

I tend to regard them as messages or
signs from departed beloved ones. Maybe
saying "hi" and to remember them?

Many cultures believe in the symbolism
of white butterflies to carry messages
from heaven, angels and deceased.

White butterflies are a symbol of hope
and transformation, indicate you are
about to start a new chapter in your life.

It is considered a positive sign, perhaps
response to prayers, angelic support and
God sees your good work. Spiritual messages.

The Chinese believe it is the soul of a loved
one, angels are watching over you,
and you are protected.

For others it is a good luck symbol, especially
if you catch one and set it free. For some
a white butterfly is an omen of death.

Zunis say butterflies predict hot weather
or rain. The Blackfoot tribe ascribe butterflies
as carriers of dreams when you are sleep.

Native Americans believe if you watch white
butterflies' grace and beauty for a long time
they can induce sleep and spiritual change.

Overall the white butterflies that visit me seem
to be uplifting messengers. They draw my attention
to the light. They travel a zig-zag, quirky route.

Bluebird Visitors

The metal bluebird on the patio
is definitely a jay, according
to the markings seen on Internet.

The bluebirds in the garden
may be jays, but probably
just bluebirds with some jays.

I just enjoy these harbingers
of happiness whether as entertainers
as I chi sit, or messengers.

In these uncertain, hard, dark times, they
are believed to indicate things will be
brighter, to hold on and see things through.

Whatever their technical name–they
are blue my favorite color. They
alleviate the blues and fascinate me.

I listen to them squawk, unable to
detect the tone, guessing what
they are feeling or expressing.

They do not land for long before they
launch to a new site. They poke dirt,
twitch, prune, belly flop, spread wings.

I admire their energy, graceful
movements, diligence, ability
to change pace, stamina.

Like the yellow dots in the grass, these
blue dots in garden and trees, bring
me delight, hope and perseverance.

Too Many Details

After some research I think
I see mostly Western Scrub Jays.
They then say three varieties:
California, Woodhouse's, Sumichrasts.

This is getting much too technical.
What shall I call them? Bluebirds?
Blue jays? Western Scrub Jay?
I think probably jays or blue jays.

Any yellow, black-edged butterfly—
is it tiger swallowtail or call it just
yellow butterfly? Add wings' edge color?
What if I see other colored butterflies?

Do I find out what kind of mushrooms
we have? Does it matter if we
do not intend to eat them? Can I
just let them variegate the lawn?

Several flowers I identify by color–
chives, clover. Buttercups and dandelions:
two favorite yellows. Some small "weeds"
with tiny, yellow blooms invade the patio.

Two mysterious plants with purple flowers
and thin leaves poke through patio pavers
and sprawl to soften the stone. No idea
what to call them–the patio purples?

I can't identify all the flora and fauna
in our garth. The berries, fruits and nuts–
these edibles— I can name. But the yard
is not all about me and my needs.

We are just temporary stewards of the 1/5th
acre we call home. All life is to be nourished,
protected, respected. At my age I may even
be forgiven for not remembering names.

Lulls

Between breezes and movement,
I sit like a statue under cloudless
blue sky and my age temperature.

As I deep breathe chi in the quiet,
I hear distant dog barks and birdsong.
I await some actions.

During my warming, 7 solo, white butterfly
flights, one duo flying tandem right in
front of me before exiting left together.

Three birds, I have determined to be
Western Scrub Jays, continuously peck,
squawk, meet and greet, flop, fly off

in different directions to neighboring
yards, only to reconcile to the chorus
of cheeps from the rhododendron ruckus.

I can't interpret bird behavior. I have
to try to understand and cope with
human's whose actions defy belief.

In the midst of a pandemic, Trump
holds an indoor rally in Tulsa, does
not wear masks or encourage others

to do so, makes a "sick" "joke" about
if we did not test we would not know
how many cases we had. You had

to sign a waiver not to sue to go in. How
many new cases will brew? Fortunately
it was not filled. He blames others, not

his hate-filled rhetoric, attacks on justice,
environment, various groups and individuals,
bullying, self-aggrandizement, lies...the list goes on.

I shift my thoughts to floral identification
and what I need to research. Something
positive. A solo white butterfly bids me farewell.

Relaxing in the Garth

Wispy thin clouds in blue sky
as I walk to my chi chair and sit
on my blue pillow to deep breathe.

It is mid-afternoon. Birds do not
appear for a shade snack for quite
a few minutes. They're quiet. Napping?

Two jays emerge to the blueberry bush,
cheep in hush tones. They stay near the
back fence in shade. A third bird arrives.

Their tone of voice changes and they
get noisy, chasing each other under
cover. Still the tiny chirps are silent.

White butterflies seem to want my
attention. Three swoop within touching.
Some messages scribble the whole garth.

An ant climbs on the bulbous belly of
the largest mushroom. Three smaller
mushrooms huddle near without bugs.

Clover colonies and a buttercup cluster
expand. One tall dandelion in the garden.
One purple blossom on the chives.

I do not want to think of heavy things.
I want to release what hurts and join
the transitional shift toward light.

Heat beats my back without breeze.
Sun chases me from my sun shields.
I go inside, where the air is conditioning.

Browsing

Birds, bugs and butterflies briefly
browse our organic backyard. I
glom my gaze on what attracts me.

Two jays have an arboreal argument
on an apple branch before taking off
in different directions before snacking.

Two jays flash across the yard near
my chair on this sunny, summerly
afternoon in June, not landing.

I notice wilting irises, diminished
buttercups, a mushroom hugging
the trunk of the hazelnut tree.

A calico cat strolls along the fence
until she finds a hole and passes
through to the neighbor's yard.

As the jay pecks the dirt near
the fence, the neighbor starts his noisy
mechanical mower. The jay and I leave.

I go inside to browse the Internet
where I can find gaps in facts and
theories, look for what I want.

I miss browsing the grocery aisles
in a red electric cart, selecting
what I purchase, not ordering pick up.

I miss browsing in stores, art and
craft fairs, finding items to meet
my needs and uplift my spirit.

On-line I find a favorite hand-painter
who will not be at her usual fair outlets.
I order three small wooden angels.

In these turbulent confined times, we can
use all the angelic support we can get, as
we try to wing-it, when browsing the news.

Sensing Direction

Shadows come and go as sun breaks
through overcast sky on a warm afternoon.
First time I'm in short sleeves this year.

The back garth is quiet. Other-yardly chirps
heard, but the rhododendron thicket is silent.
No grounded birds seen. Some fly overhead.

An abundance of nine butterflies. Some fly
widdershins, zig-zag, bob. One lands on a
hazelnut leaf for a few minutes. Mixed messages?

The mushrooms bulge and freckle, sprinkle
with cinnamon. Still one dandelion and chive,
but the buttercup battalion gained recruits.

Two reached mid-yard amid clover clusters.
Apples redden. First organic blueberries
bobbled in my breakfast yogurt. Strawberries shy.

The garth seems to reflect my mood—shades
of darkness, burgeoning hope. Sense of direction
and landings uncertain and brief.

As I pick up my blue pillow to go inside,
a jay lands on the eastern fence. I put
my pillow down and watch. A second jay

lands on the neighbor's whirligig, opening
like a lotus. Both fly into my neighbor's
yard. Have they moved? I breathe deeply.

Transitioning

Near mid-afternoon under a cloudless
sky, I bake in my chair as I gather chi,
exhale deep, hot breaths.

A butterfly on a long, cross-lawn flight
greets me as I puff my blue pillow.
I witness a parade of butterflies,

each takes a different flight pattern,
each scribbling a different message?
From departed souls or angels?

When I sent out a vibe for one to fly
closer, to my astonishment a butterfly
swoops before me. Another close, unbidden.

Under the roof overhang shadow, buttercups
have expanded territory. Four in the sun
are the tallest and shine most brightly.

White clover do not seem to glow. They
appear grayish. The mushrooms boom
and tan, patina. Faded flowers curl.

Between hazelnut leaves, I see pears
plumping golden, apples bulging rosy.
Meager peach leaves may hide a few.

Wind-powered canopy shadows jiggle,
wind chimes jingle, pinwheel— a spindle.
Garth angels barely sway, maintain direction.

Scrub jays rush into underbrush, lost
in leaves to nap? No birdsong. Bushes
near the fence provide cover.

Everything appears to be transitioning,
just like some people and the planet.
Most things seem on the move, except

maybe the craggy, crusty, chunky,
whiskery rock wall. It holds the top tier
in place, like other walls.

Eventually old walls crumble and new
structures emerge. Some walls are
durable for centuries. Built too strong?

My gardening neighbor answers his cell
and goes inside. I get a spam call a few
minutes later, stay outside despite the heat.

When it is time to leave, a butterfly bids
me farewell. Most butterflies fly through
the yard and do not land. We're organic!

The mangling mower has returned from
his bike ride. The garth faces a grim
transition. How do I transition from grief?

Shadows and Butterflies

In 4:00 shadows, canopies lean east,
dance to wind rhythms, shimmy.
The pinwheel's shadow flickers in wind.

Eleven butterflies pass through. Two
land on an azalea and two duos meet,
circle, fly off in different directions.

The first four come south-north.
north-south, east-west, west-east.
None land, all cross-yard flights.

Only one scrub jay snacks blueberries.
No birdsong, only clanking wind chimes.
Butterflies wend in and out of shadows.

Shadows' darkness covers much
of the yard. Butterflies flit white,
The sun orchestrates light.

As a hat shades my face, sun heats
my shoulders, knees and back.
Light and dark thoughts blend to calm.

When the eleventh butterfly, casts a small
shadow from overhead, I follow its path.
Butterfly signs and messages untranslated.

I go inside uncertain as butterfly flutters,
hope to leave shadows' darkness behind,
but retain their dances.

Interrupted

Several hours before eventide, late afternoon,
I went to the backyard to go with the flow,
energize chi and spin my chakras.

Noisy jays squawk from neighbors' yards,
but not ours. I see a sparrow fly over
our roof and a hummingbird in blueberries.

Raspberries are also ripe, but strawberries slow.
Plums, peaches, pears, apples bulge. I cannot
see how the hazelnuts are doing in thick leaves.

Clouds bunch on both sides of the yard,
but clear blue sky over my hooded head.
The wind chills me, as I sit in shade.

Most of the garth is shadowed. Sun spots
at the edges. Two wind chimes jangle my
tranquility. One yard angel hangs dully shaded.

The mushroom cluster grays and shrivels
in a shaggy lawn. Buttercup revival underway.
Four butterflies flit before my busy mind intervenes.

I had forgotten my blue pillow and I am cold.
Two excuses to cut this chi session short. I dash
(for me) inside to share my book cover idea.

Several recent books are in various stages of production.
As I deal with completed books, I review works in progress.
With all the interruptions and disruptions we face,

I am grateful for any ideas how to create and cope.
Wherever I can find inspiration, I am open.
Creative interruptions are always welcome.

An Extended Stay

Mid-afternoon, July 1st I sit in the backyard
to warm soul and body under sparsely clouded
sky. I plan to deep breathe and rattle chakras.

Two fallen apples bubble the lawn. One
for Adam and one for Eve and they did
not have to pick them or share.

Mid-lawn hosts shrinking brown mushrooms,
two buttercup forerunners, (others cluster near
house) and gaps in canopy shadows.

The garden hosts a giant dandelion.
A dandelion duo tall-stalk in a small
blueberry bush. None thrive in the lawn.

I extend my stay to see if any birds appear.
I hear plaintive tweets with no response.
The noisy jays are not out and about.

The butterflies start solo flights in all directions
and lengths. They seem incapable of flying
in a straight line. Indecipherable signatures.

One lands at the base of the weathervane.
The neighbor's helicopter weather station
left its fence post. Ours remains static.

We seem to share butterflies with our neighbor.
They fly in and out, exchanging yards. One
butterfly flew from our front yard to back and returned.

After waiting for birds almost double-time,
finally a jay flies under the blueberry bush,
hidden behind tall iris stalks. I can leave.

Counting flora and fauna diverts my mind
from over-thinking, over-questioning. As
my back heats, cooling winds soothe.

The pinwheel spins, casting blurry shadows.
The canopies' shadows lolly-gag east. Time
to head inside to confront the world's conundrums.

Stealth

2:30 mid-afternoon seems a prime time
to observe the comings and goings
of the creatures in the back garth.

Birds and butterflies appear to manifest
out of nowhere and depart out of sight.
After over dozens of both, I stopped count.

The butterflies fly in all directions for
longer or shorter flights. I wish I could
translate butterfly script.

When they occasionally meet, they circle
each other for a chat, then take off apart.
The jagged flights often don't land.

The birds like the same open dirt spot
near a rhododendron and azaleas. They
often fly solo, face beak to beak, leave.

Several scrub jays plop on their bellies,
shimmy and spread feathers. When done
rest or something, shake off debris- depart.

Two brown speckled birds with different tweet,
pop up under the blueberry bush, beside a
snacking jay, silently coexisting.

Suddenly they fly off, one brown bird squawks
from the apple branch. A furtive black cat with
shiny yellow eyes, sneaks to midyard.

The cat stares at me, turns around to leave
with a yellow butterfly (swallowtail?) escort.
Soon the neighbor dog barks.

A gray mottled cat surreptitiously passes
behind me a few minutes later without bird
squeak, but followed by dog bark.

Another yellow butterfly checks out the fence line,
then leaves the backyard to the white butterfly
bunch. How many butterflies return or reside here?

I can't interpret bird tweets either. These
hugger-mugger creatures wing-it their
own style and rhythm.

I am the clandestine creature, poking
into their private domain. I am the covert
spy startling them with my presence.

Mostly they seem to ignore me and if
they are trying to give me messages,
I have not decoded them.

The mushrooms dissolve into the grass.
Two dandelions survive in the garden.
Buttercups proliferate–briefly.

Soon the sly mower will demolish grass
dwellers, may pull up garden plants
he has chosen to be weeds.

At least my undercover work is not
underhanded. I share benign secrets
of garth inhabitants as I witness them.

Backyard: The Musical

The giant garden dandelion is the lead weed,
with a buttercup ensemble shining
on a green stage. Sun the spotlight.

Wind sets the tempo for pinwheel
movements, wind chimes jingles,
the susurrus of leaves.

White butterflies script librettos,
meet mid-air for a circle dance.
A refrain throughout the show.

The solo scrub jay shakes some bootie,
struts across the garth like a Shakespearean
performer, pauses for effect.

A smaller, hyperactive bird in the blueberry
bush flaps wings and squawks for attention.
A fledgling bidding farewell?

Off stage a dog barks a jarring melody.
Perhaps the dog is the villain? No human
animals in this production, except background.

Modern touches are machine noises
from mowers, traffic, airplane.
A contrail is a banner.

The scenery is rusty rhododendron
and azalea blooms to bring modernity
to the green scene.

The musical is heard on different
wavelengths for diverse audiences.
My limited equipment misses a lot.

Canopy shadows cast shade
a finale. Some characters vacate
the stage. Ends with a whimper.

I can imagine the plot and the sounds,
as I sit on my blue pillow and silently
deep breathe chi. My feet hip-hop.

Unloved Flowers

A weed is but an unloved flower. Ella Wheeler Wilcox

If it were not for "weeds" our summer lawn
would be a plastic mat–butch cut and green.
Dandelions and buttercups are a pawn.
The mower wrecks havoc at the scene.
>Where is tolerance for diversity?
>Why must "weeds" face adversity?

Would be a plastic mat–butch cut and green
if the lawn did not have splashes of color.
I miss the decapitated heads unseen.
The yard has a greenish pallor.
>Give me sprinkles of yellow and white.
>Give me swashes of beauty and delight.

Dandelions and buttercups are a pawn
in gardener's prejudiced, judgmental view.
They reduce the grass to a boring yawn
after their disrespectful, killing is through.
>Chopped, lopped heads make me sad.
>Such violence makes me mad.

The mower wrecks havoc at the scene.
If he waits too long it is hard to mow.
Late summer he does not intervene.
Between mowings, weeds have little time to grow.
>They are slaughtered with a hand mower,
>which makes their wait a little slower.

Where is the tolerance for diversity?
Fine for people, not for "weeds"?
Such thoughts make things worse for me.
as I try to steward nature's needs.
>Wild flowers aren't tamed, but get whacked,
>line road with blossoms our yards lacked.

Why must "weeds" face adversity?
Just because someone wants their slots?
They deserve a verse from me.
I'll praise these flowers creating bright spots.
>I love dandelions, buttercups and clover.
>I'll miss them when their season's over.

164

Peek-a-Boos

My right eye sports a black pirate patch
from cataract surgery yesterday. I spy
the backyard with my good, uncovered eye.

Two butterflies play peek-a-boo from
behind the weathervane base and another
from behind the chive cluster.

Orange flowers emerge from some unknown
plant. Buttercups unfurl under the roof shadow.
A pinkish peach peeks between some leaves.

Three fallen apple domes bulge in grass.
Butterflies land in strawberries which
birds shun for hiding in a blueberry bush.

The wind pushes the pinwheel from clarity
to blurry blades. Invisible fingers play
the wind chimes in sporadic rhythms.

Leaves conceal and expose branches.
Airlika angel hangs on a hazelnut limb,
draped in shadows, lacks luster.

Tootsie, the weathervane angel toots
her horn on a wave length I can't hear.
So many peek-a-boos I cannot detect.

Vibrations from other dimensions leak
through, so we hold many frequencies
within us? How do we tune in?

Little brown jobbers select a barren peach
branch to survey the yard. Two blue jays strut
in the garden, sneak into the rhododendron.

A dog barks and another joins in beyond
the wooden fence. The wind chills me. I take
some deep breaths for my invisible chakras.

What I can see is fleeting, transitory. Even
when I can see with two eyes again, I know
many peek-a-boos will be missed.

On a Lazy Afternoon

Mid-afternoon on a cloudless day,
my sun-warmed chi chair with blue
pillow welcomes me to sit awhile.

The backyard has no birdsong
and infrequent wind chimes. The
back neighbor seems to be talking

on his cell phone, as I only catch
tidbits of his chat, but hear no response.
Three blue jays in a procession, overly

socially distanced, prostrate on the garden
mulch, spread their wings. Pray to an unseen
deity for safe flights and tasty repasts? Power nap?

Regenerating solar splash? Tanning? Dumping
some waste? When done, they flick their feathers
and return to the underbrush. They matched sky.

Few of the white butterflies land. Most
pass on to neighbor's yards. They seem
to manifest from air. Disappear out of sight.

Three fallen apples plopped in the grass.
One green-sheathed hazelnut dropped
at my feet. Lots of buggy folks.

Two buttercup scouts reached midyard.
The small colony remains tucked under
the roof-line shadow, like fireflies.

Two tall dandelions lurk in the azaleas.
At first I did not see them and thought
dandelions had gone extinct in our garth.

Despite one eye patched, I did eventually
discover them. When I went inside the proof
to Grounded with Gaia arrived. Spirits revived.

This lazy afternoon gave me a respite from
heavy headlines, achy body, blurry vision—
some glimpses of hope.

Scrabble Squabble

Mid-afternoon I head for my back garth
to absorb some chi, rattle chakras, contemplate
the debate of using offensive slurs in Scrabble.

My wooly mammoth-ish jacket is topsy-turvy,
hood between legs, back to toast in sun.
> Why not a hyphen tile for hyphenated words?
> How about punctuation? An interrobang?

Bird chitter and butterfly flitter may have meaning,
but I cannot transcribe bird or butterfly language.
> Some Scrabble players have cut 200 terms
> from their lexicon. Word meaning over points.

Two butterflies rendezvous in the strawberry patch,
rise, circle dance–converse? Off in separate directions.
> When I play cooperative Scrabble we don't
> count points. Seek out new words to use.

A spider drops an invisible line from the hazelnut
branch, like a period or inkblot to my thoughts.
> Scrabble players do play by rules. If some
> words offensive, I vote to not accept them.

A new tiny purple plant pokes through the grass. I do
not know its name. Proper nouns excluded in Scrabble.
> There are 192,111 playable words used by player's
> association. Hasbro wants experience inclusive
> and enjoyable for all. Meaning overrules points?

Butterfly distractions flutter my concentration. Flaming
orange flowers intrude on green. Grass gobbles up mushrooms.
> Since I play competitive and cooperative Scrabble
> by different rules, in both settings I favor discovering
> new words, dislike counting points, use dictionaries.

My three surviving dandelions are called weeds. They may prefer
being considered flowers. To me whatever language is used,
be respectful, slurs and profanities are not.
> If in doubt, leave it out? Just points, not messaging or tact?
> I can't wait to play an in-person Scrabble game to use
> the word garth and my mother's nickname Honey.

Summer Speculations

My back warms with the setting sun,
as I sit late afternoon in the backyard,
a respite from a noisy, chaotic world.

White butterflies visit, some land
in the strawberry patch, but most
just wave hi and good-bye.

A blue jay emerges from the rhododendron
bush for a blueberry snack and to splat,
wings out in the garden bark dust.

A smaller gray-blue bird eats blueberries,
which must have been a big gulp, then
moves to the spiky, orange flowers.

Buttercups, clover and a small purple
plant, lower than the mower, embroider
the lawn, left to dehydrate until fall.

Dandelions banished to the garden
grow tall. Beacons of light I check
on daily, hoping they haven't vanished.

Peaches and apples pink up. Plums
and pears ripen as well. One green
hazelnut sheath reject at my feet.

Three planes and three sirens interrupt
contemplation to more dire thoughts.
Wind chimes faint in light breeze.

Few pinwheel spins. The temperature
the same number as my age. Shadow
stretches to the east rock wall.

Childhood summers we feared polio,
my grandparents survived 1918 flu.
Grandpa made wooden coffins.

Schools this fall might be virtual.
Foreign students might not be able
to attend colleges and universities.

All the viral uncertainties in addition to
climate change, social justice, pollution
can make one feel daunted.

When shadow creeps over me, I leave
my blue pillow on the chair. A fruit fly
follows me in and bugs me at my computer.

Butterfly Time

At five
I go to sit
in my backyard, witness
flora and fauna in waning
hot sun.

Two small
grayish-blue birds
visit orange, spiky
tall stalks.

One jay
emerges from shade
of rhododendron for
brief garden stroll. Today
I watch

for white
butterflies whose
haphazard flights intrigue me.
Two dash before my face, exit
to left.

The white
butterflies fly,
but do not land, like a
dragonfly on orange, flaming
flower.

Un-mowed
lawn seeds clover
clusters, musters the freed
purple plants and the buttercups
to spawn.

Above
it all the white
mothy flights zig-zag in
tepid wind chime wind, limp spins of
pinwheel.

Today
I hope on white-
winged bandages to heal
disease, destruction, division
on Earth.

Black Butterflies

Midday I went to the backyard
to sun-soak for my balmy, cloudless,
summer, chi-gathering ritual.

For the first time I saw not just one,
but two black butterflies amid the float
of usual white butterflies.

White butterflies are supposedly good
luck, souls of deceased, symbol angels
watch over you and protect you.

I've seen yellow butterflies infrequently,
but do not recall seeing black butterflies.
Do they have myths and symbolism?

Once inside, I learned black butterflies
symbolize new life from old one, but
subtle after a period of transition.

Black butterflies indicate change,
transition, freedom, rebirth, death of
bad things and misfortunes.

Some believe witches transform into
black butterflies to steal food. Must
be dieting to shrink so much.

The Aztec war goddess Itzpapalotl
transforms into an "obsidian butterfly"
to devour souls during a solar eclipse.

A black butterfly can represent power, evil
authority, elegance, sophistication, fear,
anger, sadness, death, mourning, remorse,

the unknown and mystery. Guess it is open
to interpretation. I like seeing diversity in our
garth. Perhaps transformation is my best hope?

Summer Quarantine

Without stirring abroad,
One can know the whole world;
Without looking out of the window
One can see the way of heaven.
The further one goes
The less one knows.

Lao Tzu

Displacement

Sometimes, feeling 'out of place' can be terrifying. But if we are never out of place, we can never share our differences nor use them to bring us together. Experiencing something new can help us create so much more and better. Sometimes, light must be displaced for us to see the beauty, the rainbow. Ardea C. Eichner

Our normal routines have been displaced
by COVID-19 and protests for justice.
Follow new guidelines as old ones erased,
the old ways of living will not suffice.
> Leave old normal behind for a new way.
> Be cooperative, sustainable. Let past decay.

By COVID-19 and protests for justice
we find ourselves in uncertain times.
We must work together and sacrifice
to heal and redirect handling of crimes.
> No one should be hungry, homeless, bullied,
> under-educated, find their health care sullied.

Follow new guidelines as old ones erased.
Wear masks, social distance and wash hands.
Pass new laws on how police hands are placed.
Make sure everyone is treated fairly, understands.
> These traumas fall on minorities and poor,
> more than the privileged with a wealth detour.

The old ways of living will not suffice.
The inequities are too hard to bear.
The displaced have had to pay a higher price.
These game-changer events make people aware.
> How long must we wait for leaders to emerge,
> to make positive changes so hope can surge?

Leave the old normal behind for a new way
which includes diversity, equity, unity.
Must we wait for 5D to arrive, interplay?
Don't let the predators escape with impunity.
> Kindness and respect must prevail.
> The violent and unjust should go to jail.

Be cooperative, sustainable. Let past decay.
The future of the planet and living beings is at stake.
Our best intentions must proceed without delay.
Can humanity withstand another preventable mistake?
> As we deal with a pandemic, peacefully protest for change,
> can we hope and dream for a better, creative exchange?

A Saturday Pandemic Drive

On a rural ride through farms and forests,
wild flowers rim the road–orange poppies,
Queen Anne's lace, Scotch Broom.

Meadowfoam covers the hills white.
Orchards with grapes, hazelnuts,
almonds, apples. Corn and grasses.

No buildings for long stretches.
A few cows. We spent an hour viewing
wide spaces, cocooned in the car.

We ate lunch from a drive-thru
in the car, munching in the parking
lot. Cars social distanced.

He ordered, wearing his mask.
I put mine on as well, then
we pulled them down to eat.

It is Memorial Weekend, so we
stayed away from main drags.
We did not plan to stop or get out.

When we returned home, we placed
our masks to be washed. We breathed
filtered air in enclosed quarters.

Thoughts on a Rainy Ride

*We delight in the beauty of the butterfly, but rarely admit changes it has gone
through to achieve this beauty.* Maya Angelou

We break out of our Covid cocoon and drive
to the Cascades and the flowery median strip
of Sweet Home near Foster Lake.

Wind glides big raindrops up the windshield.
Even in a rural respite ride from disease, death,
protesting, cocoons open, phase 2 emerges.

We must make our metamorphosis, before we become
butterflies. Pundits proclaim we can emerge from
this trauma better or worse, hope conditions improve.

Humanity faces climate change, racial, sexual,
economic, educational, health care inequities.
Disease and the death by police of an unarmed man,

alert us to what the privileged have denied others.
Anger at injustice has erupted. An incompetent
President holds a Bible upside down in front of a church

he does not attend for a photo op, clearing protesters with low
helicopters, sprays, projectiles, pushy police. He enrages
the priests and the fed-up public, he can't lead or care for.

He barricades and barb wires the White House, goes
to his underground bunker. Nearby on the street, protesters
paint in giant yellow letters Black Lives Matter.

When I return home to gather chi and look for white
butterflies–I wonder if they are big moths? When will
the diverse splendor of other colored butterflies appear?

Under a Strawberry Moon

And when it rains on your parade, look up rather than down. Without the rain, there would be no rainbow. G. K. Chesterton

During my first massage in several months,
we celebrated the ascension of a full moon
lunar eclipse–the Strawberry Moon.

Things are supposedly going to look up
for us all. With all the whammies lately
some light portal downloads are welcome.

Mid-afternoon is overcast, with rain
predicted in a few hours. My body is
refreshed from the massage, chakras clear.

My hatless, unruly hair fizzes in the breeze.
Buttercups march west toward mid-yard.
Chives and irises blah, past their bloom.

The azaleas and rhododendrons are
withered crones. A brash blue jay darts—
bullseye into the later's underbrush.

The breech brings a screech from
another jay–more of alarm than welcome.
An incessant harpie still yips after

both join a third jay in the garden. Duos
squabble beak to beak, flash feathers, meet
on the peach limb, depart back to the garden,

peck the rock wall, one follows another
to the sideyard- still shrill. I have no idea
which two are bickering. Are they mating?

It does not seem so, but in the privacy
of the sideyard–who knows? One lands
on Tootsie, the weathervane angel.

She stands firm. I look up at Airlika angel
hanging dimly from the hazelnut branch.
Pinwheel whips its blades. Wind chimes noisy.

Between the bird's chirping, turbulent wind
setting things into a fury with faint canopy
shadows–I've had enough and grieve inside.

At the Clinic

As we walk to the clinic's entrance, the
line extends beyond the pickup overhang,
curves down the sidewalk in the rain.

Red tape marks social distancing and
masks are required to enter. Only one
person to take your temperature.

He rolls my wheelchair to the side under
cover and stands at the end of the line.
I watch the soggy people inch forward.

An elderly lady with a walker is confused
by the line. A young couple let her cut in.
She says she has had surgery.

A mother and her teenaged son are in
front of her. The mother talks constantly
on her cell phone beside her silent son.

She is clueless about the large gaps she
causes by her inattention and all the people
who have to stand in rain longer. I speak up.

I tell her to move forward. She does, but
since she is mask-less, she and her son
are stopped at the entry and handed masks.

My temperature is 95, my husband's 96.
She comments I must have been chilled
waiting to get in. No lines inside.

After check-in it is moments before I get
my B-12 shot from a pink-uniformed nurse.
I take off my hoodie to my short-sleeved,

red BAZINGA tee shirt. There are no lines
at the elevator or leaving the building. It was
lucky we were early coming, as I usually am.

I am relieved to take off my mask in the car.
My glasses often fog, but I am clear why I
must wear one. I do not go out except

when I go to the clinic for appointments.
It will probably still be too rainy to sit
outside to mull over world's health issues.

AARP has a phone call Town Hall with
our Representative Peter DeFazio. He
gave a speech and took questions.

Since it was AARP sponsored, most
of the concerns were about medicare,
health care, high drug prices.

Legislation is underway, stalled, likely
blocked. Our nation does not give its
citizens protection from pharma predators

or provide healthcare for all, like most
nations. I know that, just as I know
the protests about George Floyd

are not just about police brutality,
Black Lives Matter, but societal
inequities in education, employment,

justice, discrimination and health care.
Normal is abnormal and must be improved.
We need more clinics for mental health as well.

The Methodical Mower Strikes Again

He starts to push his man-powered Fisker
in the front yard first. People (who are not
staying home) could see his dandelion warts.

No one but us has been in the backyard
for months. Why can't he let me have yellow
in the lawn and a little scraggly green?

I sit in the backyard. Sunny day. Shadow
shade fades and darkens under a contrail
scarred, white-cloud-puffed sky.

A buttercup beside my chair pioneers
mid-yard with a few others, blazes the trail
for a horde of buttercups to the east.

Aggressive grass swallows mushrooms.
All the flowers wither and brown–even
the small red rose bush looks depleted.

The birds are off their snack schedule.
I glimpse a jay hiding in the blueberry bush.
Strawberries and blueberries bulge unseen.

Fluffs of puffball waft by and settle in the lawn.
I hope for dandelion revival. Then mangler man
comes to the backyard with a white weed pail.

He says the front yard is hard to mow, since
he had waited two weeks. He is "cleaning up."
As he nears the purple, patio plant and grabs

one of its vines I say, "Can't you leave anything
alone?" He leaves empty-handed after his one
compulsive pull. Metal bluebird still wreathed.

He returns to the front yard and I am able to
stay in my sanctuary in peace to gather chi
and warm my back. But where are the birds?

My red Andean hat a stop sign? Two white
butterflies, minutes apart, appear. The pinwheel,
angels and wind chimes barely, rarely move.

I go inside before the massacre begins. There
is too much killing, asserting power over others.
In this reality is there sanctuary? How long?

The First Day of Summer

Pandemic spikes in several states.
Food distribution to children glitches.
Food bank lines are hours long.
Opinion on toppling toxic statues switches.

SCOTUS made some good decisions.
POTUS holds a dangerous rally.
Protests for equal justice continue.
Unnecessary deaths continue to tally.

Meanwhile there is climate change,
defective leadership, casting blame.
We stay at home, wash hands, social
distance–except Trump–he brings shame.

Division multiplies. Even day is overcast.
So much uncertainty, lies and pain.
Summer vacations altered. Unemployment,
disillusion, breaking dreams again.

You can't watch screens or read the news
and not have your heart break.
Such incompetence and hatred
is very hard for us to take.

I make lists of what I'm grateful for.
Many remain very abstract.
I wish I were amid the protests again.
I'd like to make a bigger impact.

When will humanity not disappoint,
be responsible, kind, generous, caring,
work for truth and justice. To do so
requires commitment and daring.

Seaward

We're out of the valley, over the coastal mountains
to the sea on a summery, clear day despite
forecasts of weather grayer and chillier there.

Road rimmed with towering conifers, wildflowers—
daisies, dandelions, Queen Anne's lace, poppies,
white and purple lupin, I resisted picking.

The winding road to Walport has little traffic,
many tourists flock to the ocean. Drive-thrus
had long lines, sit-in restaurants few diners.

Small towns en route had several vacant
stores. At the coast craft shops are scarce.
Several fudge shops, but not drive-thrus.

Views of the sea with shiny waves crashing
on rocks. Signs indicating you were in or
leaving a tsunami zone were unnerving.

One seagull, one bluebird, three butterflies
on the journey. The wind was cooler and
stronger at the coast. Open windows refresh.

Many people wear masks, even downtown
Corvallis at the Saturday Market. Fewer
lupin from Newport to home. I wish

I had lupin in my backyard. When I sit here
I see more scrub jays skirmish in the blueberry
bush and underbrush, pose on a weathervane.

White butterflies land, after scribbling their
message, like a period at the end of a sentence.
Usually they pass-thru. They could be big moths.

Though I can't always name what I see, wherever
I am, I appreciate beauty, movement, ocean waves—
respites from chaos and turbulence.

Naming

Swedish botanist Carl Linnaeus named
a small, sticky weed after a scientist
he disagreed with.

What could we name or rename Trump
that is not real estate? Confederate statues
tumble down, why not a fumble down for Trump.

Maybe we can try to erase Trump's image?
Maybe we can not re-elect him–not that we
really did elect him by popular vote.

I'd really have to dislike something to call
it Trump. Trumped up means fraudulently
concocted, spurious. Sounds appropriate.

It is an ugly sounding word with ugly
associations. Maybe I should not impose
the name on anyone or anything.

I may not know the names of some birds
and plants–even people, but I do not call
them Trump. He bumbles along at our expense.

We need to be aware of the connotations
of the names and words we use. I just hope
Trump get trumped by integrity and justice.

A Virtuous Weed

What is a weed? A weed is a plant whose virtues have not yet been discovered.
Ralph Waldo Emerson

What if there is no such thing as a weed?
Weed meaning marijuana is virtuous to some.
Even if it is just beautiful, what is the need
to have virtues to make it winsome.
        I don't mind the most pesky flower.
        People, not weeds, make me glower.

Weed, meaning marijuana, is virtuous to some—
used medicinally for it alleviates pain.
Some claim it is addictive and worrisome.
Other smoke pot again and again.
        CBD cream on my arthritic knees,
        take away my soreness, please.

Even if it is just beautiful, what is the need
to judge it a nuisance, in the wrong spot.
What deep hostility do you heed
when you decide it must go, why not
        just revel in its touch of color.
        Find another viewpoint to explore.

To have virtues to make it winsome,
must it be edible? Have many fans?
Why have you made some plants unwelcome?
Do they interfere with your gardening plan?
        Can't you revise to be more inclusive?
        Must you weigh virtue to be conclusive?

I don't mind the most pesky flower,
its wily, wild, defiant attitude,
makes me a tolerant grower
for they perk up my mood.
        But then I don't "weed" or prune.
        To their problems, I'm immune.

People, not weeds, make me glower.
Their virtues are on trial,
as they destruct hour by hour.
Others watch in denial.
        Be more protective of weeds,
        this weed-enjoyer pleads.

Calm on the 4th of July

The meticulous mower placed my chi chair
on the eastern edge of the patio, giving me
an unobstructed view of the garden.

Our neighbors' over 75 foot maple is
not obscured by the hazelnut canopy.
It flails in the wind like a flirty skirt.

I'll watch TV fireworks later, but while
the sun shines and it is quiet, I will
try to calm amid the pandemic.

One swallowtail flies among white
butterflies. One scrub jay hops
up the three power lines for takeoff.

Another jay dives into the rhododendron
which appears to be a hideout or
nesting place for tweeting jay visitors.

Humans are color-blind compared to birds,
who can see four dimensions of color,
as opposed to humans who can see three.

I wonder how our backyard looks to birds?
Human eyes attune to red, green and blue light
and mixtures of those, see mostly spectral colors.

With many gurus suggesting we are shifting
toward the fifth dimension, will our color
palette be enhanced as well?

According to Lorie Ladd, she channels
all is well and things are unraveling as
planned, as we shift to higher dimensions.

She had some suggestions to stay calm
in the midst of upheaval, darkness, anxiety.
We can try these tips to stay calm in chaos.

When I gather chi and tweak my chakras
in the backyard, I am trying to raise my
consciousness and assist a shift.

First we must visualize ourselves in
the center of a storm, remember
the bigger picture of the shift.

3D density is becoming 5D light.
Observe the lens you choose to see
external reality, use higher consciousness.

Try not to judge. Observe and be aware
and go with the flow. Stop and pause
anxiety, anger, rage and fear.

Settle into the body and deep breathe,
then push play and go again. Turn
off external stimuli which is nerve-wracking.

Turn the volume down, go inside, quiet
the chaos. Shut off and come back calm.
Remain in the eye of the storm.

Even five minute breaks can help. Turn
off TV news and violence. We are moving
toward ascension. Try to remain calm.

All these massive shifts globally with climate,
health, societal change, can drain a soul.
While we are staying home, social distancing,

masking, washing hands–perhaps we can
make some time to calm down, let the future
unfold and cling to the hope all is well.

I leave my blue pillow on my chair and
go inside. Tonight I will watch fireworks
on TV at a safe distance, concentrate on

beauty and not on the air pollution, the
clueless unmasked, crowded people.
We are in need of a higher consciousness.

Saint Corona

A local Mennonite wood carver makes
wooden statues of saints. Because
of the coronavirus, he chose St. Corona.

Since there are over 10,000 saints
and I am not Catholic, I can probably
not have been expected to know of her.

Corona was a 2nd century married teenager.
Victor was her brother-in-law who refused to
renounce his Christian faith at Romans' request.

Court judge Sebastian under the reign
of Marcus Aurelius imposed a death
sentence. Corona prayed for him at his side.

Victor was beheaded, but Corona was torn
in half, limb to limb. They tied two palm trees
to the ground, tied her, released trees to split her.

Over the centuries she was a powerful witness
for prayers for resisting plagues, also patron saint
of treasure hunters, not just epidemics and pandemics.

The Coronavirus is a killer, but by less violent means.
Some blindly refuse masks, social distancing, hand
washing due to some misinformed beliefs.

Praying to St. Corona might comfort some people.
Any source of relief from these uncertain times is
welcome. I'll stick to dark chocolate, cock-eyed optimism.

Mid-July

Half of 2020 is over and most was spent
in a global pandemic with no end in sight.
Poor leadership from our President.
No cures found to fight this plight.
  We stay at home, wear masks,
  social distance, wash hands–small asks.

In a global pandemic with no end in sight,
people are fearful, sick, sadly divided.
No country seems to handle COVID-19 right.
Not enough hospital equipment provided.
  People want normalcy to return.
  Old systems crumble and burn.

Poor leadership from our President
causes unnecessary deaths and delays.
Such denial, he's just incompetent.
We're victims of his bullying, greedy, ways.
  Will people vote in their best interest?
  Too many think the POTUS knows best.

No cures found to fight this plight,
no vaccines, just shutdowns.
We're in a war we don't know how to fight.
We'll see where responsibility is and who owns.
  The economies tank, many unemployed.
  Gone the amenities many enjoyed.

We stay home, wear masks
when in an enclosure.
Masks protect others. Tasks
performed at home. No closure.
  I like seeing colorful patterns on faces
  when I am in public places.

Social distance, washing hands, small asks
when so many will be protected.
In the backyard bare-faced I will bask,
warm chi and chakras with rays collected.
  No gatherings to visit or meetings to attend.
  Isolation might pay a big dividend.

Disillusioned

On a cloudless, contrail-less early afternoon,
I plop on my chi chair pillow and hope to heal
my sore neck and three frozen nose sunspots.

The newly mowed lawn spawns brown patches,
but no bright colors. Not even clover! I call
for the mower to show me survivors.

He points to a small dandelion in the garden,
a tall dandelion beside the compost heap,
and five tiny, earth-hugging unseen buttercups.

Soon a white butterfly waves a quick howdy.
It would be an hour before three others stopped
by from the west. None of them landed.

Despite some peeps and rustles in the underbrush
of the rhododendron, no birds appeared before I was
ready to leave. Then one jay in bulging blueberry bunches.

A new bushy "weed" behind the chives had thin
limbs and tiny pink buds. One deep pink rose
huddles near the back fence. Hard to detect.

An ambulance siren, two planes, gentle wind chimes,
a neighbor's whistle, a dog bark break my bubble
barrier. I am disappointed at the lack of color and action.

The mower picks ripe plums, he has picked up apples
before mowing. The two peaches are out of reach.
He plucks buckets of blueberries almost daily.

I sit a long time sun-soaking, hoping to see some
pinwheel spins, Airlika, the angel on the hazelnut branch,
sway. Tootsie, the weathervane angel, rarely budges.

As we stay at home, interacting with pages and screens,
many crave fresh air and promise of nature. We have
not stewarded the planet well. I deep breathe, go inside.

Remembering

Love unlocks doors and opens windows
that weren't even there before.

Mignon McLaughlon

Who Are You?

Can you remember who you were before the world told you who you should be?
Charles Bukowski

Supposedly, our DNA codes our innate being.
A blank slate after we are born? Then how
are we to know our cosmic mapping?

If we have many lives in many places,
how does this current incarnation factor in?
This Earth experiment is designed by what forces?

To figure out our place, religions, cultures,
theories, families all impinge on us, tell us
what they want us to be. Does anyone know?

I am told I picked my parents, made a life
chart with challenges for my individual growth.
Spiritual, physical, mission? How do I access it ?

If my chart is erased...why? How does that help?
It's hard enough if guidelines are provided.
Rely on angelic intervention? What is truth?

Seems I am continually making choices,
judgments, guesses what might assist
my own and the planet's progress.

It is not all about me. Like coronavirus, I
can asymptomatically impact others. I can
self-quarantine, but I'm always, on my own.

Humanity is a quirky, sometimes unkind
experiment of dark and light. We label
each other, blame, reject responsibility.

How are we to cope and hope when we
do not understand our purpose to be here?
Just another cosmic joke, to entertain...who?

Are we Recorded in Akashic records, a "cloud"?
An illusion? Hologram? Just go with the flow?
Unanswered questions. Counterproductive suggestions.

Am I a starseed? Light-bringer? A Pleiadean
Blue Ray? Ruled by instinct? Lured by pleasure?
I don't remember knowing who I am or supposed to be.

Pondering 80

Tomorrow I'll be a longevous crone,
sheltering in place during a viral shut down.
At least I'm not celebrating alone,
but probably no candles blown.
        I'm content staying inside
        with brief chi-chair sits outside.

Sheltering in place during a viral shut down,
doing my part toward social distance.
Pandemic mishandled by orange, whacky clown.
Not confident in leadership in this instance.
        I am a most vulnerable corona target,
        but all ages get ill, don't forget.

At least I'm not celebrating alone.
My husband is with me, takes good care.
We contact others by computer or phone.
We try to update, prepare and remain aware.
        We try to cope with what each day will bring.
        We transition from dark winter into chaotic spring.

But probably no candles blown,
for we'd rather eat pie than cake.
We'll have a delicious meal on our own.
I'm glad I don't have to bake or make.
        Lovely cards come through the mail
        and thoughtful notes over email.

I'm content staying inside,
writing and reading, watching TV.
I know I must ride with the tide.
Try to keep fear from overpowering me.
        I worry about world and beloved others,
        all the good actions the virus smothers.

With brief chi-chair sits outside
I replenish my energy, watch nature,
breathe the renewal of spring, decide
what creativity and intentions to nurture.
        I cherish each warming, sunny day
        and hope the virus soon goes away.

Reading the News on My Birthday

The local paper and New York Times
share very little good news.
- Coronavirus stats continue to climb.
- 6.5 millions Venezuelans leave children behind with ill
  relatives and young siblings to seek work. Children prey to
  violent gangs, sex trafficking.
- Locals stranded in Peru, can't come home.
- Medical equipment shortages dire. Staff sick.
- 1.3 billion Indians in lockdown...

I skim for bits of good news before starting
my day. Eat my crispy bacon treat.
- I'll fold the paper to close out news.
- Place the paper out of sight.
- Try to concentrate on good news and deeds that will
  happen today.
- Thank the paper delivery staff who created the paper and
  delivered it.
- From self-quarantine it is one way to keep in touch while
  social distancing.

This Easter

This Easter the United States is under
a national disaster declaration as deaths
from coronavirus and cases are highest
in the world. The Pope says Easter's message
is hope in difficult times. Temples, churches
and mosques are closed this holy season.

This Easter in quarantine with my husband,
we will not make Easter baskets or prepare
a family gathering dinner. We connect
by phone and email. We have not gone
to church in decades, so no change there.
I do have Cadbury mini-eggs in a drawer.

This Easter is sunny and warm. I will
put on shoes and go into the backyard, try
to inhale chi, attempt to connect to my highest
self and the cosmos. As a multi-dimensional
being, I might become aware of divine
intentions beyond this 3D reality and illusion.

This Easter will be very secular for me. I will
not debate or judge Easter's foundations.
Any efforts to lighten the darkness are welcome.
If we are governed by a cosmic code, with almost
digital cosmic connection and are programmed
by an unknown source, do we have any free will?

Stellar Jay Amid Holly

As the
fog lifts, a jay
perches on holly branch,
no hurry to feast, fluffing its
feathers.

Jay seems
to see me, but
the window shields us from
contact. This bird does not attack
window.

Unlike
the visitor
who banged-head at bush's
reflection, this bird hangs on branch
tightly.

We sit
and stare, wonder
what each other perceives,
see who stares the longest. Focus
human!

The bird
has enough of
such nonsense and flies off.
Holly berries safe for day with
no birds?

Window
basks in sun, shines
undisturbed on this Earth patch.
Sun stokes Australian fires,
scorches land.

The jay
has local threats,
but in my front yard some
respite from danger, lingering
in peace.

Living with Choices

Those who have a "why" to live can bear any "how". Viktor Frankl

In rehashing my choices, regretting the
paths I took, is really not productive.

It is not that at this stage I could handle
switching choices. I've not the energy or
mobility. So why do I reflect harshly.

Perhaps I feel I did not achieve my goals.
I let others' needs overcome my own.
I placed my happiness in others.

As a result I have been very hurt and
disappointed. If I had made other
choices would it have been better?

The old mustard seed of wisdom to know
the difference... If I were more gifted, I
think this lifetime would have been different.

I have been told what my life purpose is.
Was I guided in this direction? Did I really
have much choice? Just acting the script?

I have always felt loosely attached to this
planet. I have always imagined elsewheres.
I have always chafed at earthly expectations.

Being a woman coerced by cultural pressures
I find confining and unsatisfying, has not
consoled my multidimensional uncertain soul.

Now in shut down, able to write as much as I want,
reflect too much on what never happened and what
did, words can't express my "why".

Bubbles

In my self-quarantine bubble
I go to gather chi on my chair
in the backyard near a hazelnut tree.

It is around four and overcast.
Earlier sun took lawn shadows.
It is windy, sky tinged with gray.

Full blooming red rhododendrons
and azalea complete with a lavender
rhododendron and chives.

Five dandelions align behind my office
wall. Others social distance around
the lawn, some puffballs ready to seed.

I had been reading my journal from 1970–
fifty years ago when at 30, I had recently
driven across country to Oregon, towing

a travel trailer with two young sons
to their father's job at Oregon State.
We bought our first and only house.

I wrote the "bubbles of life break in my hand."
I suffered from feminine mystique. My
circumference limited, but less than now.

I've blown and popped many bubbles over
the years, but my heart breaks for younger
me with so many dreams still out of reach.

Today, no butterflies. One jay on the power
line flies to back neighbor's yard. A side neighbor
squeaks and squeals shrill baby talk to her dog.

I reminisce among a spinning pinwheel, clanging
wind-chimes, inert replica angels, tangled
lawn with floral fringe, mossy tree trunks.

I would love to burst this pandemic bubble
bubbling all over the planet. I hope I can
keep my fragile bubble intact, blow new bubbles.

In Memory of the Cherry Tree

There is a huge mole on the face
of the lawn. A two-foot diameter
dirt blemish in the clipped grass.

It is at the site of the chopped
cherry tree, whose rotted remains
left a hole to be filled.

Soon it will be a grass-covered grave
like all the others without a tombstone.
Gone, soon unremembered.

How long before lawn swallows
the dirt-filled dent? How long
before the mower forgets it's there?

When there was a stump left, you
could see the wound. Soon no scar.

Mother's Day

Late afternoon on a sunny, warm
Mother's Day Sunday, I carry my
blue pillow into my backgarth.

I sit and gather chi, reflect on
motherhood and the roller coaster
ride it has been of joy and sorrow.

A cacophony of birdsong greets me.
Jays appear from the roof, rock wall,
peach, apple and hazelnut branches

during my sit. A sparrow on a spindly
peach limb scopes the neighborhood.
A big black ant crawls over my shoe.

Two white irises bloom near the back
fence. Neighbors' newly-white azalea
blooms peer through a wire fence section.

Eventually three butterflies flit by.
One over my head. Buttercups
doubled to over four dozen overnight.

Despite all the distractions, I am not
uplifted, my back's not hot. Tears run
down my face. The gentle breeze

may be enough to spin the pinwheel
and ring soft wind chimes, but the wind
does not dry my tears or whisk them away.

I have communicated with my two living
children today, but it has been decades
since our son died at nineteen.

His ashes nourish a tree on a hill in Oregon.
His tombstone is with his grandparents at
the family plot in Connecticut, as they wanted.

It does not matter, he is not here or there, and
I couldn't visit during this shutdown. So I grieve
as mourning doves coo and the sun sinks.

I carry my blue pillow back inside. Every
Mother's Day is a jabbing reminder of
the son who can't show up.

My Mother's Hands

My mother's hands had age spots,
wrinkles, gnarled fingers from arthritis.
She was very vain about them
and tried to keep them out of sight.

My mother was very creative. She
loved crafts and interior design. Her
gardens especially cherished sunflowers.
Despite illnesses she did most chores.

She wrote letters to me weekly.
Somehow in a move they were lost.
She remained homebound mostly,
unless her son drove her in later years.

Needlework became increasingly
difficult. Many of her pieces
hang on our walls. In one I'm
in a cradle surrounded by angels.

She did not type, use a computer,
bike or drive. She was hands-on
for writing and art. She could
reproduce objects as if photographed.

Our oldest son when very young
held her hand and stroked it.
"Does it hurt?" he asked. My
mother was touched almost to tears.

Later in one of my dreams, I
visited my mother in her living
room. She was beaming as she
exclaimed "Look at my hands!"

They were without blemish.
She looked quite young as well.
My son worked at a desk nearby.
My mother and I held hands.

At eighty I have my mother's
spotty hands and wrinkles, but
my arthritis has not twisted my
fingers. One is a little crooked.

Still my hands remind me of hers.
She accomplished a lot despite
being homebound like I am now.
She perfected family farewell hugs.

Summer Before College

Summer before college was a time of transition.
Despite scholarships and acceptances, to choose,
I could not go where I wanted to go. In a position
where lack of parental support means I lose
       my hopes and dreams at a vulnerable time.
       I had an alternative route to climb.

Despite scholarships and acceptances to choose,
I couldn't even apply to my first choice.
I would attend Central Connecticut College, my muse
would have to carry on there to develop my voice.
       I graduated in three and one-half years.
       First in freshman class it appears.

I could not go where I wanted to go. In a position
of yearning for Columbia in New York City.
My parents were in total opposition.
I had to commute. I'd worked hard. Self-pity
       was a burden I carried for years.
       I was kept near home by parent's fears.

Where lack of parental support means I lose
the best place to grow as teacher and writer.
Not in a family with student loans to peruse.
I adapted and become a feminist igniter.
       In graduate school I had better courses
       and worked my way through on own resources.

My hopes and dreams at a vulnerable time
took another twist as I broke up with high school sweetheart.
Two weeks later on my only blind date, a new time-line.
I meet future husband, date through college and start
       a long term marriage and family
       despite not attending favorite university.

I had an alternative route to climb,
I could not perceive that summer before college,
a future as wife, mother, activist with sometime
as teacher, novelist and poet, gathering knowledge.
       I never have visited Columbia or enrolled.
       It's still a great place, I've been told.

333

As I was about to get up from a nap,
I looked at the clock. 333. I need
to research its significance.

When we see three of the same number,
some believe it is an angel number
trying to send you a message.

I look up 333. Universal energy surrounds
to guide and support me, promotes creativity
and magic, urges to me to expand my abilities.

333 is a sign of freedom, encouragement,
assistance and communication, protection
of mind, body, spirit by divine beings.

Ascended Masters stand by. It is a time
to take a decision, trust and expand my
unique abilities as part of a universal plan.

Sounds like in this shutdown I should open
outward, figure out how to serve and to create.
I have over 3000 angels in my collection,

who bring me smiles, color, beauty, inspire
me to pay attention. Now ethereal counterparts
want me to step up, look up to strive up.

Therefore, I await the communication aspect,
as to how to do this. Is this part of the fifth
dimension transition? It's hard for Aries to wait.

Remembering Cinco de Mayo

The day after the 50th anniversary
of Kent State protest against war,
Cinco de Mayo commemorates a war victory.

Celebrations for both tamed by COVID-19
gathering restrictions. The colorful
Cinco de Mayo parties, parades, dances

enjoyed by many besides Mexicans could
be cancelled. Few made a pilgrimage to Kent
State. Other holidays and events close down.

My mother, of Swedish descent made
colorful ornaments of Mexican folk art
to hang on a small tree.

She decked out card tables with theme
colors, strewed Mexican figures around
the house, gathered family for a feast.

I still have the paper, hand-drawn ornaments
which I have used as Christmas decorations.
I will not be celebrating Cinco de Mayo this year.

I will stay home. Dine simply. Question violence.
May we emerge from this a more equitable
world of peace to celebrate colorfully, joyfully.

Mount St. Helens Eruption
40th anniversary May 18, 2020

In 1980 after months of steaming
and getting ready to blast, it did.
I remember hearing a faint boom.

We were in Corvallis, little ash,
but in Portland, some wore masks.
Ash took a cross country tour.

We drove north to a baseball game
but had to turn back home. Our
windshield wipers swiped ash mud.

Again we are wearing masks
against a viral, unseen attacker.
We could see the eruption's debris.

In both cases I have remained safe,
so far. I have a small ash sculpture
with tiny pink feather made from eruption.

What memento from this eruption of fear?
The mountain is recovering. Hopefully
soon the world will be recovering also.

Ironic April 6th

April 6th has several National Days
to honor certain items and events.
This year they seem somewhat ironic.

Jump Over Things Day. Now as we
are confined inside, what are we to jump
over— furniture, leap frog, hop races?

International Sports for Development
and Peace Day. We've postponed
the Olympics and most sports events.

Hostess Twinkie Day. In this pandemic
this seems trivial. How are we to get
them in germ-ridden grocery stores?

Siamese Cat Day. Why not all cats?
Or dogs? Just pets or animal day?
Guess the 6th I will not celebrate.

Still we must find ways to celebrate life
in the depths of darkness and disease. Each
of us can choose, create our own celebrations.

Lightening Dreams

The last Full Supermoon of 2020
shines through my bedroom window
above the tall holly canopy.

I stayed up very late in the hope
I could see the glowing globe
without cloud interference.

When I fall asleep, I dream
of parties, parades with unmasked
joyous people in Berkeley.

Obviously another time-line
and place with unknown people.
My dorm room is 207.

Despite convolutions of details
and feelings, I awake wondering
what meaning I can glean.

The impact is a sense of celebration.
Did I time travel to when we are not
shut in and virus-free?

I awake at 5:55 an angel number.
I do not remember the dream I have
when I return to sleep.

Dreams can present information
and guidance for our life paths.
So I looked up 207 and 555.

207 means the end of major life
cycles and beginning new ones,
developing spiritual abilities.

207 represents adaptability, balance,
harmony, spirituality, inner wisdom and
intuition. Maybe a dimensional shift?

555 also indicates a significant change
is coming– freedom, travel, exploration.
Perhaps the lock down will end soon?

555 as an angel number indicates
big changes, individualism, personal
freedom, non-attachment. Freedom rings.

Why did these numbers stick with me?
Why was I curious to check out their
meaning? Cosmic connections?

Washing Windows

Fingerprints on windowpane
        smudges of mess,
                blur and design.

Memories of when children
        pressed the glass, eager
                to go outside to play.

Cleaning windows is a chore,
        I delegate, but keep memories
                of the finger printers.

Memorial Weekend Sunday

As people visit beloved military graves,
New York Times publishes 1000 names
of COVID-19 dead, I go to the backyard,

place my chi chair in a sunny spot,
plop my blue pillow to commemorate
the living and deep breathe some chi.

Red in rhododendrons and azaleas
is leeching. White irises and chives thrive.
Even about a dozen buttercups survive.

One buttercup stands at the base
of the ladder. One buttercup, mid-yard
invites a bee to dine. No dandelions.

A fast-whirring-winging bird in the hazelnut
tree must be a hummingbird. Scrub jays
dart and peck the garden, hide in bushes.

One jay perches on the peak of roof, other
jays fly onto apple, hazelnut and peach
branches. Tootsie, the weathervane angel

hosts a jay on her back. When the jay
takes flight, she moves from north to west
before re-orienting north again.

The wily weeder returns from his bike ride,
pulls a few tall grasses from the garden
and wall, then takes a nap in the shade

of the hazelnut tree on his back. I watch
him sleep as does a jay on the rock wall.
The jay leaves when he snores.

When he wakes, we go inside. We have
family calls to make. I took the TV remote
outside with me instead of mobile phone.

My mistake kept me from disturbing images
and intrusive phone calls. Outside our yard,
people wear (or don't) wear masks. Social distance

(or don't) on reopened beaches and parks.
Soon 100,000 dead. Wars on disease and
enemies cause mourning, tragic deaths.

Delayed Gratification

It is Memorial Day. I sit
in the Moon Room, our
enclosed outdoor room
amid Christmas decorations.

They have been up for probably
three to four years. We decided
to take down the wooden spiral
dowel tree hanging from the ceiling.

My husband Court invented the design
and built it of dowels, mathematically
spiraled, to highlight each ornament,
not lost in needles like a live tree.

Hundreds of hand-made ornaments
dangle from the round branches.
My mother, brother and I exchanged
new additions for decades.

Each of us had a distinctive style as
we created creatures from imagination
or imitation. My mother and brother
were meticulous reproducers.

Mine were from my imagination.
My father, husband and brother
jig-sawed the shapes. My mother,
brother and I were the painters.

In graduate school Court and I
made a few extra to sell, to make
a little money during those tight times.
I treasure all the ornaments and memories.

We aged out of the artwork, but my set
remains up longer than the rest–sometimes
for years before I mummify ornaments in
baggies, put in a box and store them in a closet.

As I gently bag each ornament, I remember
the maker and the Christmases we spent
together and apart. My parents and brother
are dead. Pandemic keeps apart the living.

What Is This?

Emerging from a nap, I heard
a male voice say "What if this
all comes crumbling down?"

The voice came from the room
we call heaven, as over 3000 angels
from my collection are hosted there.

My husband was on a bike ride and
would not return for awhile. I was alone.
In quarantine, am I hearing voices?

What does this refer to- the collection,
my reality, the country, the planet?
What is causing the crumbling?

Wearing my blue and white donkey,
pants, my Bernie shirt and Macchu
Picchu hat, I head to the backyard.

First day without a sweatshirt or hoodie.
Warm enough to air-dry my hair. The
hat, worn like a mask, protects my face.

The brim tucked under my glasses
which fog a little, works until I place
it on my wild-haired head.

What crumbles? The red and pink
azalea and rhododendron blooms?
The mown "weeds" and mushrooms?

The peach, apple and hazelnut trees are
beginning to produce nubbins. Two white
mushrooms reside near the hazelnut trunk.

Mid-yard one buttercup and one puffball.
When the wily gardener comes out to
scoop goop out of the gutter before next

rain tomorrow, he pulls some rock wall
grasses, tosses the puffball on compost and
ignores the buttercup away from its cluster.

Small brown birds–smaller than sparrows
land at a niche in the rock wall. They take
flight and loop back to same rock outcropping.

Spring is crumbling into summer. But the voice
implied something more ominous–the increase
of disease and inequity, decrease in law and order?

What if "this" means the shift from 3D to 5D?
What if the crumbling leads to something better?
Who chooses and crumbles whatever "this" is?

Big Top

Somehow in my dream I organize
a Big Top contest to find the biggest
hair. Is that circumference? Length?

In the dream-fuzz I recall seeing long
spikes, bouffants, afros, big braids and
bulging buns. One hairdo down to knees.

Perhaps this idea came from my lack
of a haircut, due to months of quarantine—
bangs over eyebrows, wild tussled hair.

Yesterday I had been researching the holocaust,
many prisoners and soldiers hair shorn. Hair
was a product, a past luxury, a lice haven.

When I look in the mirror to tame my
sleep-tossed, unruly hair, I am not concerned
it is white, thin, scraggly. My thoughts

are not with dreams, grooming, but what
new, much needed protests, unjust deaths
reality presents today. Hair is irrelevant.

Juneteenth

Today is a celebration of freedom,
marred by a pandemic and police brutality.
Hopefully we will overcome and change.

As I head to the backyard to inhale some chi,
it is sunny, hot, just days from summer solstice.
The lawn is a yawn after moving.

Devoid of color diversity and butch-cut,
I search for escapees. One vanguard buttercup
mid-yard leads only six survivors.

The one white mushroom I can see is uprooted.
A few white clovers hover near the wall. Such
a bland carpet. I look for birds and butterflies.

Five butterflies sign in. Each its own signature?
Each signifying a different message? One
swoops near my head–urgent or showoff?

The cast of three jays appears. White bellies.
A brush of brownish-pink on their blue coats.
They chase each other, take a snack break,

talk a squawk in flight or grounded. One jay
flies near, over my head—curious, but confident,
I don't move much or interfere in their business.

Perhaps they have a nest in the rhododendron.
I hear scratchy and tinier voices like young
birds watched by older ones. Noisy visitors?

They fly by so fast, my head's like the pinwheel.
No wind chimes this doldrums day. I am listless
from a nap, massage and global bombardments.

The warm sun heals or brings nose cancer? Under
my red Andean hat, I try to protect myself. The
purple plant in the patio pavers remains.

Small yellow flowers creep over stone and soften
the pavers. When birds and butterflies leave
the stage for a few minutes, I go inside.

Hopefully somewhere there are Juneteenth parades,
rallies, barbecues, songs and dances. We need these
celebrations to spur our spirits to be free from despair.

Dual Celebrations
    Father's Day & 59th Wedding Anniversary

After a rural ride and nap, I head
for the backyard to reflect on
the two celebrations today.

It's sunny and warm. I breathe
deeply. Who will show up via
butterfly to congratulate us?

Seven white butterflies appear,
one swoops in front of me. One
yellow with black edges butterfly.

If you are a departed soul wanting
wanting to bring a message, can you
choose the type of butterfly?

One black crow flies overhead. Two
blue birds–Stellar jays? Blue jays?
They peck the dirt side by side,

sometimes touch beak to beak, screech,
take off in different directions from the
garden. They may nest in the rhododendron.

No celebratory wind chimes or pinwheel
waves. Pandemic celebrations more
low key. We wore masks for drive-thru

and did not get out of the car. Now in
our sanctuary, we review cards, phone
messages and emails. We have faced

hard times before. But mostly we have
been lucky. When I came inside, without
the walker, he held the door for me.

Each day is a gift. I'm grateful for such
a kind partner. I'm really curious who
is the yellow butterfly wishing us well?

In these uncertain times, I wish I
understood the celestial messages.
I guess I have to wing-it.

Contrasts

Yesterday we drove the 63-mile forest road
Aufderheide National Scenic Byway–
from Rainbow to Westfir and Oakridge.
> Today I sit in our cultivated,
> manicured, familiar backyard
> to deep breathe some chi.

Yesterday the clouds intermixed
cumulous, stratus, nimbus with
contrail striations.
> Today same blue sky with
> puffed clouds with gray bottoms.
> Both days in the 80's.

Yesterday towering Douglas Fir and cedar
cast shadows over the road. Road Bumps
catapulted us once to almost the car roof.
> Today the fruit tree canopies stretch
> across the butchered lawn. Pretty
> puny beside the glorious giants.

Yesterday wild flowers hemmed the byway—
purple lupin, daisies, Queen Anne's lace,
spiky red flowers like firecrackers.
> Today it's clover clusters, buttercup
> battalions, a few remnant dandelions–
> a few orange flames like red ones we saw.

Yesterday the forest was silent. No animal sounds,
quiet crows and shadowy birds, a few butterflies
managed to escape our windshield. Buggy.
> Today two small birds meet at blueberry bush.
> Many butterfly scribbles, no landings. Two
> circle dance and flit off in different directions.

Yesterday the murmur of the engine, partner
conversations, no radio. Eyes focus on sides
of the road's green splendor. Blue River below.
> Today two dogs bark, neighbors prepare
> a barbeque, children squeal. Wind chimes
> softly intermittent. Pinwheel whirs.

Yesterday people fished and swam as mountains
soared above. A sense of freedom and wildness.
fascinating patterns, sporadic campground signs.
      Today no one in my space. A butterfly breached
      social distancing by swishing past my face. It
      is a familiar scene with minor variations.

Yesterday we missed the sign to Constitution Grove
of gigantic old growth. We had seen it years ago,
but now we will take another trip. We return to valley.
      Today no signs to go anywhere as we stay home.
      The spruce is our tallest tree, many feet taller than
      our fruit and hazelnut orchard. Wilderness another day.

Yesterday in the Cascade mountains, mostly foothills, vistas
exposed large lakes, tall peaks and burns. Traffic modest.
Very curvy, roller-coaster road of surprises and delights.
      Today in the valley our backyard is organic and tamed.
      Pops of color and texture welcome—moss, lichen,
      rock wall, floral displays. We can see distant mountains.

A Soggy Day

It's a soggy day. The backyard
is mushy, greening lushly.
Unrelenting gray skies scowl.

I resist putting on shoes to moosh
through the grass to my wet chi chair.
Rain-breaks are brief, unpredictable.

Through a wall of windows framing
the currently wind-less scene, I hear
distant bird chirps, but no wind-chimes.

The pinwheel looks like a striped flower.
Yard angels just hang out, take a nap.
No thirsty essences to be seen.

Through the gap-toothed fence,
the back neighbor's light sparkles
on a sun-less day. Some tiny shine.

A scrub jay jitters through hazelnut branches,
lands to parade at the patio's edge, flies to roof
and power line–uncertain where to land.

Does the jay greet the inanimate metal blue
jay, staked in the patio pavings? Did the jay
notice Bottom, concrete angel glistening in rain?

A whisk of wind spins the pinwheel, too wimpy
to jangle the wind chimes. I will not wait
for weather changes to go outside.

Snug in my inside chair, under the afghan,
I observe window frames, creating still lifes.
For a while I am not engulfed by the world.

Open the Curtains

Open
shuttered curtains
keeping out cold, sun.
Let the show begin, entertain
the light.

Dolphins
swim in Venice
canals. Air pollution
reduced during shut down,
Zookeeper livestreams a wild dance
with fan.

Dancers
dance in the street.
People exercise on
driveways- six feet apart,
balconies ring with singing all
in sync.

Music
from phones and screens,
comedies lift our mood.
New ways to handle curtains to
open.

We must
let in the light
amid viral darkness.
Global boundaries breeched as
we heal.

Open
curtains, windows
protect, but we must see.
Shelter the windowless, expose
healing.

En-Masse

From mountaintops to crevasses
gather the masses,
the lads and the lasses
from all different classes
put on clear-eyed glasses.
Try looking-glasses.

Confront the jackasses
creating morasses.
They taint our repasses
burn forests and grasses
pollute water and air with gases
mine land for metals like brasses.
There are no free passes.

Time to unclass.
Outclass.
Take on the brass.
Alas
amass
before hour-glass
of climate change surpasses.
Kicks our asses.

Windows on the World

The window metaphor has a long career
in the history of art and in fact
in the evolvement of the human perspective
in general.

H.J. Krysmanski

Skyview

During the pandemic, when so many
people stay home, don't travel, don't go to work,
satellite images show less pollution. Any
ideas how to connect, form a new network?
    Bird migrate north late this spring.
    Planes fly less, which is a blessing.

People stay home, don't travel, don't go to work.
Caved indoors they do not see clearing sky.
Some are fearful they will go berserk.
Too many unanswered questions as to why
    virus droplets float in the air.
    So many people remain unaware.

Satellite images show less pollution, any
progress with reduction may not last.
This virus is mysterious and uncanny.
It continues to spread globally and fast.
    The sky without its gritty bits,
    now carries unseen virus hits.

Ideas how to connect, form a new network,
create more air waves, add to the "Cloud",
innovation could provide another perk,
instead of thickening a shroud.
    Rain cleanses, sun warms.
    Weather helps and harms.

Birds migrate north last this spring,
flying long distances with less gunk in air.
Harbingers of spring, hopefully bring
a better climate, end of virus everywhere.
    Birds socially distance in our backyard.
    Mostly land solo. Their journey's hard.

Planes fly less, which is a blessing.
They carry contagion and release pollution.
Many of their victims are convalescing,
while others await a vaccine solution.
    The sky surrounds us from vast space.
    The sky holds the future of the human race.

Stepping Up

I hope in the years to come, everyone will be able to take pride in how they responded to this challenge. Queen Elizabeth

The Queen had a captive audience as
many of us are sheltering in place. Most
folks are being responsible, social distancing.

Many are caring for others, helping
shut-ins get food and medicine. Stepping
up the front steps and knocking on the door.

Others take tiny steps around their home
to make confines comfortable and safe,
seek information by page or screen.

Will we take pride on how we stepped up?
All together we can dance, make our steps
count. Poignant acts of kindness spur hope.

We must step up our pace. Catch-up
when leaders fail to lead. We'll step up?

Economy Over Lives?

> *Policy-makers now must put on their "big-girl and big-boy pants" and decide between the "lesser of two evils". Do we try to save more lives or our livelihood?*
> GOP Rep. From Indiana Trey Hollingsworth.

> Lt. Gov. Dan Patrick of Texas called on grandparents to sacrifice themselves to save our economy.

> Glenn Beck said he would rather die than kill the economy.

All these conservative Republicans would rather
restart the economy than stay home and kill more jobs.
Economy or loss of life? Always government
position between loss of lives and jobs, our "way
of life" put over the people who live them?

We have a BIG boy in the White House who
wants authority over everything. But the state
governors claim they will decide when to release
restrictions and coastal regions will consult.
Grandparents hold lots of the money to spend
once the economy opens up. Keep all safe.

The COVID problem is global. The other countries
are trying to save lives as they all strive to protect
their healthcare workers with adequate equipment.
Trump's mis-guidance lead to fatal delays. He's
a grandpa–maybe he should sacrifice his office?

This might be our chance to make changes
in our way of life to be more inclusive and equitable,
provide health care, education and opportunities.
Focus on climate, sustainability, kindness, cooperation.
Our way of life has many fault lines.

Taking A Break

I need a break from human antics,
the suffering, the ignorance, their news.
People appear prone to panics,
over-sharing good and bad news.
      People have murky intentions,
      full of illusions and pretensions.

The suffering, the ignorance, their news
even in self-quarantine penetrates walls,
sad headlines, worrisome broadcast blues.
Numbers pile up, hope to plateau, malls
      empty with unemployment and virus rules
      keep social distancing—ignored by fools.

People appear prone to panics
as uncertainty causes some to lose their grip.
We feel helpless when in pandemics.
We can't escape by taking a trip.
      We are stuck in place if have a home.
      Homeless have germy streets to roam.

Oversharing good and bad news–
heroes of kindness, essential workers' courage.
Scientists struggle to find medical clues.
Politicians find others to disparage.
      Inequities reveal the dispossessed,
      privilege of greed-obsessed.

People have murky intentions,
deliberately misguide for their interests,
eliminate environmental extensions,
exterminate, when they are the pests.
      They are going low not high.
      Innocents are going to die.

Full of illusions and pretensions,
leaders display their hate and greed.
Far from resolving global tensions,
we find ourselves in dire need.
      I'd like a better place to relocate,
      to find a new planet to reincarnate.

Earth Day
    50th Anniversary   1970-2020

Once upon a time there was a planet called Earth
in a far out arm of the Milky Way.
People disrespected and degraded her worth
making for a less sustainable stay.

Climate change raised her temperature.
Pollution poisoned air, land and sea.
It became harder to balance and nurture
all living things and humanity.

Then came the COVID-19 pandemic,
a global problem needing resolution.
Divisions of ignorance, scientific and academic,
caused delays in any solution.

Too many people. Too few resources.
Too much inequality. Too much greed.
Too little data from reliable sources.
Poor food distribution. Too many in need.

The first Earth day they celebrated with parades.
People were hopeful and protections passed.
With more challenges, their enthusiasm fades.
Weak leadership and good laws don't last.

This year in shut down, in self-quarantine,
standing at least six- feet apart,
no gatherings to celebrate, they stare at a screen.
Some limit circumference around the heart.

Engulfed in plastic, pesticide and waste,
floods and droughts things are out of whack.
They dawdled too long. They must make haste
for future generations to have a stake.

It is the youth like Greta Thunberg who carry
the burden. Elderly bask in "good old days".
Many folks are unaware or are weary,
abandon hope, unwilling to change ways.

May the next 50 years (if they survive)
find them working together, as one.
If all living beings are to thrive,
they must change course–everyone.

Gaia's Spring Cleaning

Stay home people. The planet
becomes wilder and cleaner.
Animals roam into cities and towns.
Less air pollution from a greedy gleaner.

Around the world tourists see sites
without a smoggy screen.
Kangaroos, pumas, coyotes, goats,
monkeys join the urban scene.

The air will kill fewer people now,
as pollution levels drop.
Wild animals expand their habitats.
Until the pandemic stops?

Weeds, weather patterns, insects,
noise, light pollution change.
We've whacked the Earth system.
What practices will we exchange?

While we stay indoors, impact less
we see what life used to be.
People have made a mess, pay price.
Earth restores its undimmed beauty.

May Day

May Day can be a festival of spring.
Dancers hold streamers from a maypole
in the center. I remember dancing.

May Day is a celebration of workers
around the world, stemming from harsh
conditions of the Industrial Revolution.

Mayday is the international distress call.
This May Day encompasses all the meanings
as we fight to control COVID-19.

But many of the dancers will not able
to dance together unless gloved,
masked and six feet apart.

But many of the workers are unemployed,
the businesses closed with uncertain
re-openings. Many can't pay rent.

Many fear mayday. This May first when
April showers are supposed to bring May
flowers, many lives are not blooming.

But there is Regulus, brightest blue star
in the constellation of Leo the Lion,
the 4-star group looking as one, a sickle,

or upside down question mark to see
after sundown. Leo was our beloved
departed son's birth sign, so mourned.

With so much loss to contemplate,
I will look up at Regulus. In my mind
try to turn the question mark over,

flatten its curves into an interrobang,
find bursts of light in a dark time,
and hope things will look up.

Windows on the World

As we cocoon behind closed windows
waiting to become butterflies
to fly through open windows,
we can create a new world.

In this time of reflection, we can
decide if we want the old world of greed,
war, planetary destruction, be united
or divided, choose peace or conflict.

We can change the climate and our
intentions to be more sustainable, just,
cooperative, green-oriented, equitable,
clean up our messes and express love.

We see the breakdowns in our policies,
huddled at home, masked in public,
social distancing to avoid contagion.
When we are healthy–then what?

Will we take the responsibility to make changes?
Will we build a new world of kindness,
sustaining constructions, together for all?
What has this shut down taught us? Open?

Imagine

We do not need magic to change the world; we carry all the power we need inside ourselves already. We have the power to imagine better. J.K. Rowling

We might have the capacity to imagine
a New World of equity and peace,
but we need an empowering engine
to push us forward, for magic to increase.
>Followers require good leaders.
>Positive actions need heeders.

A new world of equity and peace,
a sustainable utopia is a dream.
Dark forces' grip must release.
Unattainable it would seem.
>Hard to remain optimistic
>when so much is pessimistic.

But we need an empowering engine,
some creative minds to guide the way,
some uplifting ideas to shine
and hold darkness at bay.
>Imagine a world filled with light,
>kindness, justice, and delight.

To push us forward, for magic to increase
we invent new protocols and paradigms
for the Old World ways to decease
to create a path for New World times.
>The eternal struggle of good and evil,
>light and dark, saint and devil.

Followers required good leaders
with good intentions and processes,
a team with skillful cheerleaders
to bring sustainable successes,
>progress with diversity.
>triumph over adversity.

Positive actions need heeders
to listen and sift through science
and not be fake news breeders,
take responsibility, build self-reliance.
>I dream of a magical, compassionate Earth.
>Together we can replenish our garth?

Red Nose Day

Comics,
celebrities,
musicians perform for
homeless, hungry, and endangered
children,

support
for causes that
improve children's lives with
food, shelter, safety, education,
health care.

Red Nose
from a clown face.
They are entertaining
to bring smiles and better lives for
children.

They thank
good people who
serve and help improve hope
in a troubled, traumatic world.
Thank you.

World Turtle Day

May 23rd is World Turtle Day,
a global event to conserve
and protect turtles.
We need to find a better way
to honor and serve
as they face hurdles.

Seven species of sea turtles left
six of them facing extinction.
They choke to death in plastic waste.
They are bycatch, bereft
of breeding grounds, face the distinction
being endangered by climate change haste.

Leatherbacks travel 3,700 mile trek—
threatened sea to beach to reproduce,
for a place to lay their eggs.
Coronavirus came to wreck
UN Global Ocean Treaty to introduce
ocean sanctuaries, conservation begs.

When pandemic-paused people come
out of their metaphorical shells,
they can aid marine life survival.
Greenpeace would welcome
any support, as urgency swells
and they await sanctuaries arrival.

Unmasked Universe

I marvel at the unmasked universe. It's deplorable. Scott Keeney

Unmasked partiers on Memorial Day
crowd resorts and beaches without
regard for social distancing.

The unmasked President carries
a wreath to honor war dead. His
election opponent wears a black mask.

The pandemic requests masks to
protect yourself and others, but some
say it limits their freedom (to be stupid).

The newspaper headlines unmask
other deplorable actions, Taliban,
police killing a black man in neck hold.

Bronx is another area where minorities
have more cases of the virus, white woman
confronts black birder in Central Park.

Children go hungry and remain out
of school. Food distribution system
breaks down and food wasted.

Essential workers die on the job.
Assisted living facilities are death
traps. Staff and patients not protected.

Numbers with names add up to nearly
100,000 deaths which an incompetent
administration could have reduced.

Today we expect a SpaceX launch
to the space station. They can look
down at a troubled blue marble.

We are seeing further into space.
Is there another place where sentient
beings act as deplorably?

Mask Magic

Masks can
camouflage an
evil intention or
protect from lethal pandemic
virus.

Masks can
be Halloween
costume–scary or a
glittery mystery facial
cover.

Masks on
the job to keep
patients and customers
safe. Please, wear a mask in large crowds when in
public.

Masks can
be a fashion
statement, match an outfit,
a trikini, clear for a lip
reader.

Masks can
still wear makeup
around the eyes, make
colorful accents, dynamic
designs.

Masks can
cover facial
expressions, conceal our
feelings so we can hide behind
the mask.

Re-Imagining the World

I have concluded that together we can discover the wisdom, the fortitude and the willingness to develop strategies and actions to preserve and enhance our world rather than destroy it. Jean Houston

During this pandemic while we are in shutdown,
the inequities are more glaring in food distribution,
education, employment, health care and many
other areas like climate change–globally.

Perhaps we could ponder these issues and emerge
from our cocoons ready to fly with new ideas.
The world is sick in so many ways. Working
together we might heal and recover.

If each of us could connect and contribute
what they know best, societal changes
could begin. We should not accept the remnants
from greed and inequity. Everyone matters.

The violence, disease, poverty should not
be acceptable. The waste and environmental
degradation must stop. Start applying
sustainable solutions before it is too late.

I can imagine a peaceful, equitable world
of kindness and respect, but I face a reality
that requires more than bravery, but effective
leadership, connection and higher intentions.

Masks must protect not divide. Six feet apart
not six feet under. Don't wash your hands
thinking you can wash away the situation.
Cooperation is needed for survival.

I look back at my long life of joy and sorrow.
I would leave now if population pressures
could ease, but this is not about me. It is
about the children, my grandchildren, I'll act.

On This Rainy Day

After a rainy, rural ride to
the outskirts of suburbia,
I knew I would not be sitting

on my rain-dripping chair
to sip moist chi amid soggy
backyard flowers, grass and trees.

I chose the behind windows
perch, feet on hard green slate,
raindrops plopping on the roof.

Apparently the SpaceX launch
went off, so it's not raining in Florida.
But I am here, Oregon, end of May.

Does the Covid-19 virus hitchhike
on a raindrop and splat when it
touches a face? Slides inside us?

If I am to be present, deep breathe
chi, spin chakras, I must not be distracted.
That just doesn't seem possible.

Windows shield me, keep me social
distanced. I can't see small apples
ripening. The rain drums, numbs.

Birdwatching

Watching the birds visit my
backyard is a pleasurable puzzle.
Some bird names I have learned.

But many I cannot identify
by their coloring, size or sound.
They don't know my name either.

When Christian Cooper went
bird watching in the Ramble
of Central Park, he was an expert.

Dogs must be leashed in this area
to protect the wildlife. Amy Cooper would
not leash her dog when he asked her to.

Cooper is both their last names, but
they're not related. Christian is a black man.
Amy is a white woman. Both well-educated.

When he photographed her non-compliance,
she called the police saying he was
threatening her. She was the one out of line.

These are two intelligent people. Her fears
cost her her good job for her racist actions
and she returned her dog to a shelter.

He is back bird-watching, probably watching
out to avoid confrontations involving
non-bird coloring, size and sound.

Pet-less during quarantine, my birdwatching
remains in my backyard. Even with binoculars,
I don't know all their names. No visitors to ask.

The Protesters

The most recent protests against the death
of George Floyd are burning cities, throwing
stones–peaceful protests infiltrated by violence.

Protesters confront police and military,
expressing their outrage and fear. We are
weary of the lapses in our humanity.

Race riots are not new. Protests about climate
change, women's rights, civil rights, anti-war etc.
protesters do not like the way society interacts.

Peaceful parades like the LGBT parades, marches
with speeches and singing, sit-ins without damage
seem more effective than looting, gunfire, arson.

People protest wearing a mask during the COVID-19
virus– to protect others if not themselves. We are
attacked by so many dark energies. We need light.

Despite requests to wear masks, stay home,
wash hands– protesters are breaking all these
measures and their violence alienates even more.

I have been in several non-violent marches to
protest the treatment of people and the planet.
How can we change hearts peacefully, kindly?

So much death and destruction. How can
we learn to act justly? Humanity must work
together not against each other–or perish.

Hope comes not from the protesters, but from
the light-bringers, essential workers, kind acts,
people donating time and goods to become more equitable.

Peaceful Demonstration
    Vigil and Protest May 31st 6-8 PM Corvallis, Oregon

Over 2000 people gathered,
mostly masked, some social
distanced at the Courthouse
to protest racial injustice.
        I was not there.

People chant: "No justice. No peace."
"Black Lives Matter!" Signs like:
"Living while black should not be
a death sentence," carried aloft.
        I was not there.

This is a mostly white college town
filled with protesters against injustice,
climate change, civil rights; activists
for many good causes like this one.
        I was not there.

People of different colors spoke of
this anxiety, being fed up with the degree
of systemic racism in this country—
not just now, but since it's founding.
        I was not there.

Modern technology reveals these actions
more blatantly by cell phones and
social media. We need to be always
vigilant and stand up for each other.
        I was not there.

Protesters spilled from the lawn to street,
but did not impede traffic. They were seen
and heard. A white women's sign was a black
clenched fist. Use your voice if not black.
        I was not there.

The next day newspaper covered the event
in black and white with a photo in color.
Front page for those unable to attend to read.
Many mourned with them at home.
        I wish I could have been there.

Shambolic Times

The country is in shambles
viruses, economy, justice amuck
Demented Donald rambles,
the world runs out of luck.
  Quarantined and protesting.
  A new system they're suggesting.

Viruses, economy, justice amuck.
No safe place to reside.
I am saddened, angered, struck
by conditions outside.
  So many wrongs resist solution.
  Humanity defies evolution.

Demented Donald rambles
and babbles out of touch.
Desperately he scrambles
to keep power and much
  of his bullying behavior is illegal.
  He's acting dictator and wounded eagle.

The world runs out of luck
with climate change and poor leaders.
The populace would like to pluck
these incompetent, evil breeders.
  Humanity is nearing the brink.
  Justly so, many think.

Quarantined and protesting
tied to screens, breathing curtailed.
Activists are contesting
the laws and actions derailed.
  We are all in this together they say.
  So many have gone astray.

A new system they're suggesting
more sustainable, equitable, just.
Clear the air we're ingesting,
a new beginning is a must.
  Diversity, kind cooperation
  needed in every nation.

The Metal Canvas

Black people tend to take things meant to hold them back and turn them into things that make us stronger. Dayne Crawmer

On the fifth day of demonstrations
to protest George Floyd's death,
a black chain-link fence appeared
to keep protester's out of Lafayette
Square and away from the White House.

Untouchable National Guard troops
lined up inside the park as protesters
lobbed water bottles at them. The fence
became a symbol of living unheard,
oppressed and disrespected in USA.

Signs and art work turned the metal
canvas into a gallery, a tourist attraction.
Not the wall Trump planned to build.
Bible-holding Trump took a walk
in this park for a photo op recently.

Now he's bunkered in and orders
the fence taken down. But before he
does, protesters recover their canvasses
for marches, museums, mementoes
of a historical event they lived.

The posters declared the underlying
structural problems and policy issues
in education, healthcare, employment,
discrimination, white privilege, police
brutality, racism haunting this country.

"Even now the Old Suburban Guys
are mad now." "8 minutes. 46 seconds"
"How many weren't filmed" "Color is not
a crime." "Black lives Matter." "I can't
breathe!" "Mama!" "Please!"

"Until now, I didn't understand. Not really,
I'm sorry." "If you think your mask is hard
to breathe, imagine being black in America."
"Come together right now over me." "Raging
against the machine." "2020 vision."

Many anti-Trump sentiments expressed.
Yellow trucks carried the fence away. The
White House was called the People's House.
White evokes white privilege, power, oppression.
Maybe the house should be painted a rainbow?

The metal canvas may be gone, but artists
paint on plywood-covered storefronts and
design black tee-shirts with white lettering,
face masks. Black Lives Matter painted
on a street. Posters for the persistent marches.

The pandemic kept some people home.
But masked onlookers witnessed the event.
"As a black person, there are a lot of places
that you can't go, and this wall is symbolic
of that", said Daniel Crittenden. He added:

"All of a sudden it feels like an exciting time
and a hopeful time. It's also a sad time, but
there is always that duality in black life. There's
tragedy and triumph and joy and perseverance,
all working together. You definitely feel that here."

Globally the greedy, rich prey on minorities,
exploit the poor. Unjust practices prevail.
We need a shift in consciousness and power,
a new mentality needs to deal with the environment,
social equity, broken institutions, break barriers.

Protest for Romina

Iranian father Reza Ashrafi decapitated his 14 year old daughter Romina in a so-called honor killing, setting off a debate over the rights of women and children and the failure of the country's social, religious and legal systems to protect them. Farnaz Fassihi

As the world protests the killing of George Floyd and
shout "Black Lives Matter", who will protest the beheading
of Reza Ashrafi and shout "Girls' Lives Matter"?

In both cases protesters want laws changed whether
police or that male guardians can kill, but if a mother
kills her child she faces execution. Women's lives curtailed.

In Romina's village of Lamir, her school girlfriends lay
yellow and purple wildflowers on her grave and pray
that this will not be their fate. People everywhere fear.

As I step into the backyard toward my chi-gathering chair,
a buttercup greets me. I by-step it, look at the galloping
cluster of buttercups marching toward mid-lawn.

Four towering three-foot dandelions shelter in the garden,
under the protection of azaleas. Two small dandelions
hug the rock wall–hoping to avoid mowing beheading.

The furious wind under overcast sky, chills me. I pull
up my dark hoodie, zip up. The pinwheel is frantic.
The wind chimes clang deranged. I debate going in.

A bluebird flies to the base of Tootsie, the weathervane
angel, stuck facing north. Strong wind does not change
her direction. The jay hops down to poke around the dirt.

Another jay joins in. They circle, greet beak to beak
then go off in different directions. One hops down the
rock wall, then hops over the dandelion when jay returns.

How they all can buffet these harsh winds baffles me.
I am heavy hearted. Decapitation of any living thing
diminishes the Earth's beauty. Let each other breathe.

An Ode to Joy

I write too many poems grieving
the losses of human lives and actions.
Not knowing what I'm believing.
What are lies or truthful interactions?
      I want to concentrate on joy,
      be an optimistic envoy.

The losses of human lives and actions
provoked by violence, make us aware
of oppression, inequity, bad reactions,
provoke anger, protest, change. Beware
      of fake news, manipulated media,
      as you search for a good idea.

Not knowing what I'm believing,
while I make the best of my COVID cocoon.
What conditions can I be relieving
and will the uncertainty end soon?
      What to accept and what to refuse?
      How do I inform my muse?

What are lies or truthful interactions?
I'm a thingumajig on a whirligig.
What is illusion and abstraction?
How did I manifest this earthly gig?
      Too much suffering and stark.
      Shine some light on the dark?

I want to concentrate on joy,
birth, renewal, beauty, love.
I want opportunities to buoy
spirits and experiences, shove
      the heaviness, pain aside,
      to witness the bright side.

Be an optimistic envoy
even when all impulses resist,
stop to judge, burst out, annoy?
Find a way for joy to persist?
      I guess I'll find another mode
      than writing a joyful ode.

Plastic Rain

*1,000 tons of microplastics rain on 11 protected, remote US parks and
wilderness yearly. 11 billion metric tons worldwide by 2025 equals 300 million
plastic bottles.*

Like dust
carried by wind
and rain around the Earth,
attacks ecosystems everywhere
world-wide.

Plastic
microplastics,
new acid rain threaten
water, landscapes, impacts us all
world-wide.

Plastic
production must
lessen. We can't absorb
unsustainable products now–
ever.

Becoming a Planetarian

While pondering the blunders of humanity,
I've expanded to a planetary scope.
People protest, suffering another calamity.
As we change, do we dare to hope?
>Don't stop at being a humanitarian.
>Encompass the Earth as a planetarian.

I've expanded to a planetary scope,
because things go beyond local to global.
Events tend to develop beyond envelope,
whether political, societal or environmental.
>There are so many issues we must address,
>which put all creatures in distress.

People protest, suffering another calamity.
True and fake news travels fast.
Disease, discrimination, police brutality.
People ask how long these will last?
>We are in all this together and linked.
>Problems pop up in every precinct.

As we change, do we dare to hope?
Normal is abnormal, we can do better.
Do we have the strengthen to persevere and cope?
We have many boundaries to unfetter.
>I'm disappointed in our species,
>despoiling Gaia with our feces.

Don't stop at being a humanitarian.
All living and non-living entities need our care.
Can we become a peaceful disciplinarian?
Can we become "woke" and aware?
>We must solve problems as a whole
>and determine our helpful role.

Encompass the Earth as a planetarian.
Become a steward and light-bringer.
I aim to become a cosmicarian.
Look up, become a starry dancer and singer.
>I'm tired of this heavy place.
>I dream we uplift the human race.

Mind Control

There are no walls, no bolts, no locks that anyone can put on your mind. Otto Frank

No walls,
no bolts, no locks
anyone can put on your
mind sounds ideal, but really is
it true?

People
chose ideas
or receive them by force.
Evil thoughts can filter into your
blocked mind.

Nothing
physical can
prevent your free mind? But
what good is that if you intend
to harm?

Sometimes
conditions will
impose limits on your
actions and if oppose you still
join in.

Minds fail,
succumb to age,
portray illusions, reveal
poor judgment, filter badly,
trick you.

Otto's
daughter Anne lost
diary found and altered by
Otto. Wars kill many minds and
waiver.

If minds
were truly free,
we could have better world
if intentions good. Not in my
life time.

Riding Waves

When you are riding a cresting wave, something is creating and you feel happy.
When you are riding a crashing wave, something is ending and you feel sad.
When you are riding a building wave, energy is gathering and you feel anticipatory.
Sara Wiseman

When you are riding waves of emotion,
one after another, pounding on the shore.
You hope you surf not drown.

What motivates the cycle of crest, crash, build?
Up and down, constant flow, uncertain ending.
Cling to life rafts? Brave the sharks?

What protective gear can you wear? How to medicate pain?
Withdraw? Reach out? Help others? Alone?
How much strength is needed to swim?

Stay afloat in a boat? On the surface? Never diving?
A surfboard would be hard to master with my knees
and my aging energy quotient.

Navigating waves tugged by moon, with what equipment?
Contend with trauma, mental illness, dementia?
Riding as captain or passenger?

How long will a certain wave last? Any safety net?
Beneath or above a wave perspective?
Floundering, reaching for a life line?

Facing tsunamis? Lacy hems on the shore?
Plastic waves. Polluted waves. Waste waves.
Perpetual roller coaster rides on water, land.

"I Can't Breathe."

On any given day, they spill onto the streets, driven by fury. They march. They kneel. They sing. They cry. They pray. They light candles. They chant and shout, urgent voices, muffled behind masks.They block freeways and bridges and fill public squares. They press their bodies into hot asphalt, silently breathing for eight minutes and 46 seconds. They do all this beneath the watchful gaze of uniformed police officers standing sentry. Audra S. Burch

This is the latest version of opposing oppression.
We have had protests and marches before.
We have sought ways to be heard, make an impression.
"I can't breathe" is a well-worn metaphor.
      How do we see that justice prevails,
      despite a system that derails?

We have had protests and marches before
against holocausts, inequities, violence.
At wits end, people can't take it anymore.
They erupt and break their silence.
      How to convince the powerful few
      to give the many their just due?

We have sought ways to be heard, make an impression,
pass laws to protect environment, our civil rights,
try to free our access to expression.
Still we face our blights, up-rights, fights.
      We are tired of pushing ideas forward.
      We resist those looking backward.

"I can't breathe" is a well-worn metaphor
before lynchings, gas chambers, shootings.
History always seems at war,
with its hatred, rapings, killings, lootings.
      What is humanity's purpose on this Earth?
      What do we profess a human's worth?

How do we see that justice prevails?
Peaceful rebellion? Reforming the system?
Time to examine who jails?
Just where does this injustice stem?
      Abstract, glib answers don't cut it.
      We need detailed actions to gut it.

Despite a system that derails
tracks to progress, equality, peace,
before we embark, what are the details?
How do we constructively place our piece?
      We can't breathe polluted, germy air,
      inhale and exhale safely anywhere.

Tear Gas

Tear gas,
weapon of war,
banned for combat in wars,
but not against protestors in
U.S.?

Tear gas
irritates our
tissues and disables
breathing, causes peaceful crowds to
scatter.

Police
access to these
weapons of war on own
people — abhorrent, violent,
brutal.

Tear gas
brings tears even
when not a victim, but
watching people flee from fearful
police.

We must
ban tear gas use.
"Let us breathe!" Pepper spray
not a substitute. Clear the air!
Breathe free.

Don't Surrender

*In dark times...we want to know how deep the shadows go, and what sort of
thing awaits beyond light's comforting boundary.*   Reggie Ugwu

In these dark, uncertain times of pandemic
and the unraveling of old systems to open
and to be more inclusive, things look grim.

Coping with Coronavirus and hoping
for a vaccine, watching acts of kindness
and heroism salves the suffering.

Protesters march for equality, changes
in infrastructure of health care, education,
employment, discrimination despite pandemic.

Amid the marchers are street medics, some
professionals, but others are volunteers with less
training to be street-healers, to treat wounds.

Incompetent leadership does not get enough
equipment, enforce masks, social-distancing,
hand-washing or any infringements on their power.

The Supreme Court did support LGBTQ rights
and block Trump's attempt to end DACA. Trump
calls it a blast in face to him and conservatives.

Will we oppose wars that cause deaths as well
as disease, poverty and police brutality? Can we
breathe clean air? Can we walk safely and freely?

We must not surrender hope that hatred and violence
will not prevail. We must continue to advocate for
the planet and all beings on it, lean toward light.

Time to Panic?

I don't want you to be hopeful, I want you to panic. But I've learnt that no one is too small to make a difference. Greta Thunberg.

People are not just panicking about climate change.
There is also violence from injustice, pandemic virus.
How we handle panic is a wide range.
What approach is most desirous?
>Many think it's best to stay calm.
>Others give advocacy alm.

There is also violence from injustice, pandemic virus.
Uncertainty, pain and fear play their parts,
tend to divide into them versus us.
We end up needing to mend broken hearts.
>Can we learn to make a positive difference?
>Can we climb or reach over the fence?

How we handle panic is a wide range.
Some boil and explode, take to the streets,
break or burn, pass laws, reform, estrange.
Some use social media, send out tweets.
>I prefer methods that do not harm
>as they put out the urgent alarm.

What approach is most desirous?
Education? Consciousness shift?
Not taking risks that are hazardous?
The aim is to give a proactive uplift.
>These problems do need our attention,
>a global focus and good intention.

Many think it's best to stay calm.
Others see a real emergency.
Who will apply the balm
to the wounds of insurgency?
>We must move forward to prevent
>further destruction and malcontent.

Others give advocacy alm,
volunteer, sign petitions, donate
to supportive causes to becalm.
We can't remain passive, but innovate.
>If panic is based on fact,
>maybe it's time to act.

Elsewhere

Elsewhere there is violence, conflict.
Here it is mostly witnessed secondhand.

Elsewhere there is hurt and pain.
Here my body absorbs some as well.

Elsewhere there is disease and death.
Here the pandemic is spiking.

Elsewhere there is climate change.
Here hints of it appear.

Elsewhere there are attempts at sustainability.
Here many are trying to do their part.

Elsewhere flood and fire.
Here today just overcast.

Elsewhere protests for systemic change.
Here our town works out some kinks.

Elsewhere waste, pollution suffocate.
Here we escaped Sahara sandy winds.

Elsewhere political and social unrest.
Here we are in a bubble of some sanity.

Elsewhere there is deep division.
Here some try to listen with compassion.

Elsewhere there is widening inequity.
Here we reflect the growing gaps.

Elsewhere there is heaviness and darkness.
Here too, we need light-bringers.

Elsewhere there is love and hate
Here also. We are in this together.

Preparations

After slogging through the Sunday New York Times,
engrossed in images of pain, protest, hope,
witnessing injustice, violence and crimes,
searching for ways to heal and cope,
>I go to the backyard to clear my mind,
>breathe deeply, try to unwind.

Engrossed in images of pain, protest and hope,
I see the mower left a ruff of taller grass
around the mushroom cluster, hose like rope.
But dandelions and buttercups not spared, alas.
>Several piles of pruned branches pyre.
>Not a calming image to inspire.

Witnessing injustice, violence and crimes
amid a pandemic, self-quarantine,
still my hope for change climbs.
Some stubborn optimism still might shine,
>when I see youth protesting for change,
>in systemic injustice and inequity–rearrange.

Searching for ways to heal and cope
with altered laws, higher consciousness.
We appear we face a slippery slope,
if we can't improve our conscientiousness.
>Leaders did not act in effective ways.
>Let's hope people learn and focus sways.

I go to the backyard to clear my mind,
to seek solace, beauty, healing.
Never certain what I will find,
understand what the cosmos is revealing.
>Do butterflies bring messages from beyond?
>What about dandelions? Where can I bond?

Breathe deeply, try to unwind.
Never was good at meditation.
To what purpose will I bind?
How do I make the best of this situation?
>I need to prepare to listen, play my part.
>I need to learn and act with my heart.

Global To-Do List

The Impeachment trial is underway.
He's at Davos where economists delay.
Greta's there to have her say.

In China a horrible viral flu.
Masked people avoid crowds, achoo.
Several deaths before it's through.

In Australia fire fighters fight.
Blazes leave long-lasting blight.
A very tragic, destructive plight.

In the Middle East tensions brew.
Leaders don't know what to do.
to avoid war over latest hullabaloo.

Plasticized oceans, creatures, polluted air,
earthquakes, droughts everywhere.
climate change deniers, unaware.

People addicted to drugs, screens, cell phone,
vaping, alcohol, homeless, depression prone.
Death by despair, suicides feel all alone.

Racism, sexism, wealth inequity divides.
Opinions urge people to take sides.
Quality of life, opportunity slides.

The list goes on–stress unending.
Our future—a few are over-spending.
The rest of us are left pending.

I'd love to bury my head in the sand.
So much I wish I could mend and understand.
I can hope light over darkness takes command.

Windows on the Cosmos

Windows are a metaphor for seeing.
Every window is specific, tells us something–
not a big story, but something that becomes visible
to the outside. Above all else, windows
have permitted man to experience the essence of light
from Chartres Cathedral to the painting of Vermeer,
and to this day even the most mundane use
implies some sort of interaction with the unknown
and with infinity.

H. J. Krysmanski

Contemplating the Big Questions

Over lunch with a friend, we ponder
the big unknowable questions, whys.
We discuss what was before the Big Bang.

Is it one of many? What was there to create
a beginning, let it explode and expand infinitely?
What was before and what's next.

Is consciousness multiversal?
How was life on Earth seeded?
What force created the cosmic plan?

What is Earth's role in the cosmos?
If we are part of All, what are we part of?
Why did we choose to incarnate on Earth?

How much free will? Did we make a life chart?
Do we get a respite between lives and where?
Some of us feel we came to Earth reluctantly.

Do we have angelic guardians to keep us
on track and help us fulfill our missions?
We all could use a supporting hand.

I just find Earth's duality and darkness painful.
Somehow I feel there is a better lighter option.
I'd like my next life to be peaceful and warm.

But we find ourselves here and wonder where
we came from and where we are going. How
much is predetermined and do we have choice?

As we explore other dimensions in our dreams,
maybe we will discover somewhere else
that could fulfill our to-do and want-to-have lists.

Until then we have fun contemplating holographic
construction and illusions. Reality is up for grabs?
I am resigned to not knowing and to enjoy questioning.

Asteroid Day

Asteroid Day is a global event to share knowledge
about these leftover remnants of the birth of a planet.
Some are shattered, never-matured protoplanet fragments.

The Association of Space Explorers chose June 30th,
the day of Earth's largest asteroid impact in recorded
history–the Siberia Tunguska event.

Asteroid Day plans to educate the general public
about the importance of asteroids in our history
and the role they play in the solar system.

Scientists share the cutting-edge discoveries
from the largest telescopes and space missions.
Asteroids are considered stepping stones to Mars.

We want to learn more about the birth of our
own planet, by studying Ryugu, Bennu,
and the binary asteroid Didymos.

They are looking for resources to exploit
as well as expanding scientific knowledge.
Did asteroids bring the ingredients for life?

So much to learn. I just hope they keep
social distancing for asteroids and don't
crash Earth into asteroidal bits.

Happy 4-4-4 Today

444 is a powerful symbol of Archangelic Support 04/04/2020 (2 plus 0 plus 2 plus 0=4) Melanie Beckler

I'm a math-phobe and a letter-phile,
so I am a little numerologically and
astrologically skeptical, but in these
pandemic times, open to listening.

Apparently Archangels are surrounding
the Earth and supporting us with their
light and love. We are to be on the lookout
for blessings and miracles, opening hearts.

What are they doing other days as Earthlings
ponder their own place in the cosmos and face
overwhelming challenges and changes? I am
aware of several angel numbers 111, 222, 333...

I have seen them, but always have to google
what they signify and ponder what they might
do to me, how they relate to ALL. Today we
are to clear our mind, open hearts, tune into LOVE.

Archangels support and empower you to call forth
the highest Divine Timeline and Divine blessings
of Light and Life available to co-create through
you. Beckler suggests meditations and angel courses.

Of course you must pay for Intuitive Art Therapy,
Angel Intuition Course, Angel Solution Membership
to enhance your chances to communicate with the
higher-ups. Weren't we assigned an angel at birth?

Definitions of what is divine, angelic are murky.
So much depends on belief. How much is encoded
in our DNA? Some people have more faith in
numbers and the ephemeral than others.

But any good cause to celebrate sounds needed
in these troublesome times. What and who will come
is unknown. I'd like to believe in free access angels.
Numerical solutions? I would not count on it.

Conjuring Fairies

If we are indeed multidimensional beings,
why can't fairies be another cosmic expression,
starseeded as an earthly experiment.

Fairies are an essence of light, sustained by light,
ethereal, possible shape-shifters, grounding
like earth angels. I'm an angel fan.

If I can believe in angels without proof–unseen,
why not fairies lurking out of sight in my yard?
Some people claim to have seen fairy folk.

Delightful myths and stories about them prompt
my imagination. Since childhood I can imagine
creatures of many kinds, design aliens.

When I gaze over my manicured lawn,
with selected plantings, built walls and fences,
I like conjuring fairies camouflaging their own scene.

Perhaps they can shift density and like reported
aliens walk among us? Perhaps we are all
holograms and illusions? Truth without proof?

Musical, dancing, environmentalist fairies,
what's not to like and dream of? Evolved
between humans and angels?

The universe is not all about us. I welcome
sharing the mystery and wonder of what
may be possible. Welcome to this world, fairies.

Giving the Blue Light

Your job is to figure out what the world is trying to be. William Stafford

During this pandemic, the world is wondering
what will the future bring. Has humanity brought on
the wrath of God or is it lifting to a higher dimension?

Things will seek a new normal. Judgment
and blame are unanswerable whys. The planet
has had extinctions and cleansings many times before.

So many systems require adjusting. Climate
is on a rampage. People will migrate and borders
won't hold. Face with walls or compassion?

With movement and commerce shutting down,
innovative ideas try to compensate, people
cooperate, yet the dark side is insidious.

We are bombarded with suggestions how
to cope and hope. I like putting Christmas
decorations back up to brighten the atmosphere.

We can rim our front door with blue bulbs, electric
candles in the windows. In this time of social distancing
we can't invite people in, but our lights could guide their walk.

Do we want a world of just red, yellow, go traffic lights?
Spiritual blue lights to go with the flow? I am a dreamy
light follower. Are our white candle lights Earth stars?

Rules of Karma

*Your head will tell you a million things about how things should or shouldn't be.
Give your head a rest, and follow the rules of karma.* Sara Wiseman

Choose as wisely as you can, but also know
there are no mistakes, just soul lessons?
> *When something is completed it will go way.*
> *When something is changing it will change.*
> *When something is real, it will remain.*
The rules of karma are in effect at all times.

There are no mistakes, just soul lessons?
I guess that is a judgment call?
Somehow my confidence lessens.
Will we find a global protocol?
> What does the soul want to know this life?
> What does the soul have to learn in all this strife?

When something is completed it will go away?
Is this in our life code when we will die?
What obstacles are put in our way?
How much do we have to try? Why?
> Whatever we create goes into a "Cloud"?
> Can't certain things stay? Just await a shroud?

When something is changing it will change?
We have no free will? Just go with the flow?
Pandemics and climate cause us to rearrange.
We are afraid, suffering, don't know where to go.
> Change can renew and demolish the old,
> bring new ideas, opportunities, I'm told.

When something is real it will remain?
What was once real, will decay.
Are we illusions, tricks of our brain?
Multidimensional? Real in cosmic way?
> What is fantasy can be uplifting.
> Are we dimensionally shifting?

The rules of karma are in effect at all times.
How many sets of rules are we to abide by?
Any adjustments for different climes?
How many choices for us to provide by?
> Diversity remains and divides.
> We need help from better guides.

The Last Full Supermoon

Tonight I hope to see the last
Full Supermoon of 2020. Seems
pretty early to not have any more
this year. Ah, a burst of energy beams?

It is only the 6th of May. We are
in lock down. The weather is confused
what it should be doing, changes quickly.
I watch this indecisiveness–bemused.

I try to schedule sitting outside
when it is likely to be sunny and warm.
My timing is not always best.
Just gathering chi away from harm.

Tonight might be cloudy and the moon
unable to present its true glowing glory.
A flashlight in the sky to guide our way?
How much impact? That's another story.

Whatever lunar beliefs we might have,
and earthly ones as well,
are being put to the test,
as we watch the pandemic swell.

Pink Super Moon

Closest super moon of the year,
      seven percent larger.
Called Paschal Moon, it sets
      the date for Easter.

I hope the clouds blush
      this super super moon.
Perhaps I will see this Easter
      forerunner– like Easter egg.

On-line it looks spectacular–
      a beacon of beauty.
At its best time, I hope to see
      this spotlight on our drama.

White Super Moon

By the time I peered
at the Pink Super Moon
around 12:30, it had
blanched white.

Earlier it had a tinge
of pink, I was told, but
after midnight it matched
the sheets. Up too late hint?

I squinted with my one
cataract-free eye.
Smudges of gray amid
the pale orb- almost marble.

The ghostly moon haunted
my quarantined situation.
I had looked out for weeks,
but not gone beyond the yard.

This moon is closest it's been,
but no danger to social distancing.
Just the moon and me eyeing
the Earth with perplexity.

Angels' Staycation

If we all enter this realm
with a crew of angels and
a guardian angel in charge,
being earthbound within
the confines of a Corona cage
with an uncertain human charge
must test their mission's patience.

Perhaps they take turns
on watch and take cosmic
breaks to join other hosts
in heaven where large gatherings
are permitted? They take a deep
breath, put down their halo, before
bouncing on clouds en route back?

My guardian Bella and her crew
at my house are reminded of their
task by the over 3000 replicas
in my angel collection. If energy
is fluid, perhaps they change places
for a while so inanimates can animate
and stretch their wings? Energize them?

Energy and consciousness are
considered pervasive. Apparently
COVID-19 virus is as well. I'm sure
diligent angels will be delighted when
their Earthling is more mobile. Angels
can enjoy more cosmic flying. No being
likes to be confined against their will.

Thin Places

According to a Celtic proverb, "thin places" are where "the barrier between the physical world and the spiritual world wears thin and becomes porous" Jordan Kisner

Like the thin veil of Halloween when
some claim to glimpse the departed,
while wearing masks as every day now?

In dreams we explore other dimensions,
the thin places sleep transports us to?
We're in a cosmic alternative reality.

How is spiritual defined here? Divine,
ghostly, unanchored souls, unknown
places our imagination can conjure?

Somehow there is a leak-through
of the barrier we consensually or not
define as our experience on Earth?

Our energy and consciousness may
not have these boundaries. While we
plop on "solid ground", we travel?

Some say all that happens is recorded in the
Akashic Records. Others say "The Cloud".
They are unseen records of physical beings?

Into this vast multiverse, they want to send
robots with our memories and consciousness
to other planets. Do they have thin places too?

If we are encoded with a life chart with an
angelic guide for this incarnation (a blend of
densities), do we need thin places to communicate?

With our limited equipment, we might miss many
thin places. So many realms beyond our ken.
Heavy Earthling bodies carry light souls?

So much goes on beyond our awareness.
Thin places hold portals? Thin places conceal
and reveal if we have the will to find them?

Pondering Ylem

Ylem: The hypothetical initial substance of the universe from which all matter is derived. Word of the Day.

Like sour dough starter expanding into solids?
Ylem must be magical to be so diverse.
Imagine the unseen particles, elixirs, liquids.
Is there Ylem for each universe in the multiverse?
> Who created the initial Ylem?
> It's not just for our own solar system.

Ylem must be magical to be so diverse,
to manipulate matter for every purpose.
How much density for a multidimensional universe?
Is creator of Ylem knowable? No, I suppose.
> Does Ylem work like a 3D printer?
> Does Ylem mutate as cosmic imprinter?

Imagine the unseen particles, elixirs, liquids
as part of the flow needed for creation.
Designing planets, stars, light beings, grids
can't be a solo occupation.
> If discovered in a lab how was lab formed?
> The true method leaves us uninformed.

Is there Ylem for each universe in the multiverse?
What was the concept for the Milky Way?
Are their places to be, better...or worse?
Do we get to pick a place from a wide array?
> Maybe Ylem is just a myth?
> A preposterous concept to play with?

Who created the initial Ylem?
Many try to name this mysterious force.
Who initiated this strategem?
Will humanity ever discover the source?
> Ylem is a conundrum for human minds.
> We are fallible, the universe reminds

It's not just for our own solar system.
Why was Ylem conceived?
Is Earth a special gem
as many have believed?
> Does Ylem have the wherewithal
> to change the cosmic protocol?

Shadows in the Smoke

When you come down the cosmic chute...we are but shadows in the smoke.
Pat Benincasa

Shadows in the smoke alludes
to living in illusion, like maya
in Hinduism, a smoke screen.

My perception of reality is
we are an illusion, a hologram,
digital projection of some type.

We appear to be guided by
cosmic consciousness and
DNA encoded life paths.

Like shadows of trees, what
are we shadows of? Smoke
conceals clarity.

April was Angel Month. Will
they bring May miracles? A
shutdown planet wants to breathe.

Will the shadows of the future not
be people, but of the flora and fauna
freed from our stewardship?

Spacy

Astronomers discover exo-planets,
galaxies, black holes, parallel universes,
name telescope for Dr. Rubin.

Astrologers predict events and
influence decisions depending
on placement of celestial bodies.

While people are in shut down,
they tend to get overwhelmed,
a bit spacy with new demands.

The planet continues to orbit,
wallows in waste and pollution.
Looks to the stars for salvation?

Summer Eclipse Gateway

Eclipses are gateways that support us in entering into a higher dimension of being. Melanie Beckler

With a New Moon in mid-May, we opened
a Portal of Light unfolding in June and July
Eclipses, an Eclipse Cycle for mastery.

June 5th is a Full Moon Lunar Eclipse.
June 20th- Solstice and New Moon Solar Eclipse.
July 4th- Full Moon Lunar Eclipse.

Whether this has any significance or not,
people embroiled in the pandemic
will be hoping it is a sign for deliverance.

Believers think eclipses are triggers
necessary for life changes. It's time
to step up on multiple levels.

We can aim to align with our Highest Soul
Truth and Purpose. This is already
in the works for many people in some way.

During this period if you want to realign,
detach from the outcome and let go,
stay present, centered, adaptable,

ready for the unexpected. Release what
no longer serves you, make way for new
creative inspiration and expression.

In this uncertain, definitely unexpected time,
you might ask what you really want to manifest,
experience and create in your life.

Dream big. Bring incredible light, peace and
blessings into your life now. All this sounds
great, but the global situation requires

world-wide efforts, cooperation, uplifting
poverty, health care, education, hunger,
a just inclusive approach, effective leaders.

I do not see eclipses impacting this pandemic.
Some believe the coronavirus is God's punishment,
for our lack of stewardship of the Earth, each other.

Other's claim Jesus will protect them from
the virus and they don't need to wear masks,
with no concern who they might infect.

It is another challenge in our cosmic experiment?
Any real purpose for this added suffering?
Whatever is in charge of the cosmos, lighten up!

It is hard to be hopeful when humanity has been
disappointed, dis-empowered so often. Too many
whys unanswered. Who accepts responsibility?

We are all in this together to protect all life
and the planet. Our progress has been slow.
The pandemic provides kind and cruel options.

Tell Me Why

Why do I pursue the question "why"
when no one seems to know reasons.
Most answers do not satisfy.
Knowledge and wisdom seasons.
        I hope someone knows.
        My frustration grows.

When no one seems to know reasons
behind the questions
and intention seems treason,
there are no good suggestions.
        I'm left to ponder,
        bereft to wonder.

Most answers do not satisfy.
From what I am gleaning
many like to testify
what is life's meaning,
        but what is the foundation
        for this pontification?

Knowledge and wisdom seasons
some answers of dubious source.
Some take what's easy and "pleasin'"
without a solid backup resource.
        Where does purpose come from?
        What pattern breaks from humdrum?

I hope someone knows
where we get our sentience,
from where our creativity flows
and endows our intelligence.
        What is our place in the universe?
        Do we forget what we rehearse?

My frustration grows
as humanity tends to dominate
the planet and life. I propose
we pause to recalibrate
        what we are doing, try
        to heal and answer why.

Thinking of Jayne
    For Jayne Magras

Join me Jayne this summery,
cloudless day in the backyard.
Manifest a chair and communicate
with me from wherever you are.

You told me to rise at sunrise, face
east, barefoot, to deep breathe some
chi, looping the core of the earth
to the cosmos. I've done modifications.

I can't go barefoot due to diabetes,
and sunrise is not my gig. I'm also
a fair-weather, chakra-spinning, chi
gatherer. I'd love to cosmically connect.

You came into my life at a potato
topping potluck for writers. When
we introduced ourselves, you came over
to tell me you had been sent to heal me.

You were a world-wide healer in Corvallis
and one of your missions was my knees,
which you said were the worst you had
seen. We became friends, my knees did not.

You claimed you were a walk-in, who entered
the body of a woman wanting to exit. You
came with cosmic guides, who would sometimes
have messages for me which you relayed.

You took my life story class saying you hated
poetry, yet your first piece was rhymed. You
brought new age books to class for mostly
elderly, more conservative classmates.

You loved sushi. Whenever you visited Corvallis
after moving to Manzanita, you bought sushi
for you and your daughter Morgan. Morgan
had a daughter Felicity. You adored both.

You miraculously found funds to go to Mexico
in 2012 for the Convergence. You received
back child support payments out of the blue.
You were puzzling to many more staid folks.

You had me undergo an activation. You
said my son, Kip sent energy to his mother
from Alderbaran. You also made essential
oils which never seemed to work with me.

You said we originally came from the Dall
universe which is like a twin to the Dern
universe we are now in. We worked as
counselors in the Pleiades. Then came here.

You introduced me to points of view
beyond my usual inquiries. You appeared
a bit quirky and way outside the box, but
your generous spirit drew others to you.

You were very anti-vaccine. I wonder in
this pandemic if you would still feel the same.
What healing powers could you wield,
what guidance from your cosmic chums?

I am sure you pop in to visit your family.
Perhaps at some point I might sense
your presence and learn more of what
is to come in these uncertain, earthbound times.

As I watch winged-ones— white butterflies,
sparrows and Stellar jays winging-in and out,
I wish you could stop by and tell me all
you have learned on the other side.

Of course, you are welcome inside as well
where I spend most of my time. I miss you,
my fubsy faery, who lead me to question
the meaning and makeup of the multiverse.

Inside Out

In order to change your life outside, you must change inside. The moment you are willing to change it is amazing how the universe begins to help you. It brings you what you need. Louise Hay

This sounds reasonable, but is this always
possible? How can you change inside
to prevent bodily and societal attacks?

How can enlightening withstand pandemics, unjust
cultural mores, once they are in progress? Protest
the aftermath, support just, compassionate causes?

No matter how I change my inside physical or mental
health, the cosmos might just not help me.
Maybe I am supposed to suffer a warped world?

We can all be responsible for our actions and
contribute best we can, but if the cosmic plan
is not on board are we doomed to fail?

Where do the guidelines come from? How much
control do we have? Do we go with the flow
and hope light washes out darkness?

Humanity just seems ill-equipped to steward
this planet. It is not just people to consider.
Outside is huge for one inside spark to lighten.

Optimistically we can hope for a cosmic assist,
a dimensional shift, a DNA tweak, but as it stands
now we are in a chaotic mess with poor leadership.

As I probe my heart, brain, guts for meaningful
action, I can barely handle myself, let alone tackle
global issues with my limited resources.

I am concerned for beyond myself. I want the cosmos
to uplift everyone. Angels are supposed to assist us.
Have they retired their wings? Fluffed out in frustration?

When I search within, my inside and outside do not
align. My dreams get dashed by reality. I'm not sure
where to turn for guidance. Still I persist and resist.

Let Yourself Flow?

The Universe attracts you to the reality. This is the Law of Flow. Don't push the river. Let yourself Flow to your new reality. Sara Wiseman

Hmm. The Universe is flowing pandemic and protests
against inequality and injustice? The Universe is
attracting us to a new reality? It did this before?

The river of life ripples over rocks, river teeth.
We don't attract reality to us ? Who put in roadblocks?
How does Universe attract people to a certain reality?

Do we incarnate with a cosmic code encoded in our DNA?
The reality that unfolds for us is guided by the Universe?
How much free will does that give us to attract?

The Law of Attraction backwards? Our evolution cosmically guided?
Are the divisions, discriminations, hatreds, innate?
We need to await cosmic intervention to change?

What is the timing of a consciousness shift? Leaks flowing
into malleable minds? Are we just puppets in experiments
we did not design, but perform scripts?

Reality is seen and felt through different lenses. What determines
what beliefs we espouse? We just flow into a new reality?
Are we manipulated by disease, fear and anger?

If the Universe is attracting a reality toward me, will I drown
or swim in the flow, float a boat? Now I'm quarantined.
I'm in a bubble about to burst– confused, isolated.

Perhaps the Universe is slowing the flow, to keep us in our head
and less in direct contact. Perhaps in the polluted air,
we will see some clearing. Where are we flowing toward?

Angel Wings

An angel is a belief with wings. Tony Kushner

We can interpret this statement in several ways.
A belief in angels with wings, may be we imagine
beings with metaphorical wings for flight, which sways
into faith not logic for what is unseen.
> Angel beliefs take flight rather than grounded?
> Angel beliefs based on the ethereal unfounded?

A belief in angels with wings, may be we imagine
higher beings much like us, but with wings.
But if they don't need wings in their divine scene,
does that mean our belief in angels swings
> toward a more possible actual reality
> more in line with their actuality?

Beings with metaphorical wings for flight sways
our beliefs more toward spiritual inclinations.
Are beliefs that fly attached to angels always?
Do beliefs change with shifting expectations?
> You have angels attached to beliefs and wings.
> Are beliefs really connected to either things?

Into faith not logic for what is unseen
focuses on restricted speculations.
Angels are integral into what belief means,
but not all believe in angels' interpretations.
> Not all beliefs require angels for insight?
> Not all beliefs require wings flight?

Angel beliefs take flight rather than grounded
because of the need to uplift, find support.
As earthly burdens tend to be compounded,
some turn to deities like angels as last resort.
> Angels bring thoughts to enlight.
> Angels bring hope all will be all right.

Angel beliefs based on the ethereal unfounded?
I'd like to believe guardian angels are real.
Many angelic beliefs are pounded
by unbelievers as uninformed and unreal.
> Lofty beliefs borne by winged angels may be
> a pipedream, an escape, a delusion, a fantasy?

Celestial Bodyguards

There's a theory that Angels are born with us and every person on earth has a designated guardian Angel whose sole mission is to protect, comfort and support you in life. Angels are non-physical entities vibrating on a different frequency from us humans. Carline Gutierrezz

When Angels want to get our attention,
she suggests eight ways they might do so.

Seeing repeated patterns.
Often this is numbers like 333.

Seeing colors when meditating.
Sometimes flashes of light.

You can feel a tingling sensation
in your crown chakra.

Your room suddenly feels warmer
without any apparent reason.

Feathers appear from nowhere.
I collect them, when lucky to find them.

Dream of an Angel visitation. When you
awake have new found energy and clarity.

You receive emails and tv ads that seem
targeted to you. Synchronicity.

If you believe you are a being of light
and child of the universe, Angels are a bonus.

Harmonic Convergence 2020

From July 5th-14th a historic experiment is taking place around the world. A global meditation to invite peaceful extraterrestrials to show themselves with thousands of lightships across the sky. Why? What does it mean to have convergence that's harmonic? We aspire to collectively raise consciousness and thus planetary stewardship, by lifting humanity into deeper resonance, coherence and world peace, and beyond world peace...universal peace.
        Program introduction

A friend went to a harmonic convergence
in Mexico in 2012. People from around
the world gathered for spiritual renewal.

This experiment has a different on-line
approach with speakers and podcasts,
worthy goals and certainly needed intentions.

I have always believed in E.T.s and other
life in the cosmos. Waking from a nap,
I saw white ships, packed like sardines

outside my window–a dimensional slip?
In dreams I am dimensionally traveling.
If this works, all to the good.

Gurus advocate ascension to the 5th
Dimension is en route. Others say
we have past tipping point to extinction.

If lightships parade around the planet,
will this make people more "woke"?
Will we imbibe stewardship vibes?

Peace would be wonderful in these
violent, stressful, dark uncertain times.
I signed up to check it out. We'll see.

Simulated Reality

A growing body of scientific evidence now suggests the unthinkable–that our everyday world, and everything in our world, including us, is the result of mysterious simulated reality that began long ago. Gregg Braden

I have heard we are in a hologram,
a computer program, alien experiment.
Now they suggest an algorithms program,
an ancient catalog of what choices meant.
      Like a science fiction theory,
      Scientists have begun this query.

A computer program, alien experiment–
who knows what the cosmos has in store.
Perhaps we are making a breakthrough sent
by some cosmic committee for us to explore.
      Better up my computer skills.
      Is this a combat of wills?

Now they suggest an algorithms program
with a mysterious force with energy to place
informational photons, atoms and molecules to cram
into the mostly empty space.
      A 3000 year old codex, an ancient map of time
      details our choices from mundane to sublime.

An ancient catalog of what choices meant–
and the consequences of these choices,
challenges beliefs and paradigms, intent
to give us understanding, hear our voices?
      Does it contain keys to solutions?
      Explain necessity for our revolutions?

Like a science fiction theory
are our bodies "wired" to heal, transform
and transcend, retell humanity's story?
Will knowledge empower us beyond the norm?
      Science, spirituality, everyday life converge
      like a tapestry with mastery on the verge.

Scientists have begun this query,
finding meaning in our lives and past.
Many unexplored details in this inquiry
might indicate how long we'll last.
      I'm willing to look outside the box,
      get a new vision, break the locks.

When Dreaming

Asleep,
we slip between
dimensions, other worlds,
realities, holograms
unknown?

How do
images come?
Cosmic movies, brain blasts,
creative projections on
mind screen?

How do
we control the
content? Take what comes or
depends on type; therapeutic
vivid?

So far
I request
no nightmares before sleep
has its way with me. I hope for
the best.

We Are

We are each other's harvest; we are each other's business; we are each other's magnitude and bond. Gwendolyn Brooks

How do we describe what we are best?
A physical manifestation of consciousness?
We are each other's harvest?
We are each other's business?
  We strive for goals set from beyond?
  We are each other's magnitude and bond?

A physical manifestation of consciousness
embodied for a 3D existence?
Here to learn, to teach, uplift this mess?
React with resistance or persistence?
  Do we live many lives at once, many places?
  To discover certain beliefs our mind embraces?

We are each other's harvest?
What kinds of seeds are we?
Which plantings do we suggest?
Do we stop gardening eventually?
  How do we enhance conditions to grow?
  Who can we turn to who really might know?

We are each other's business?
Are we intruder or exploiter?
Do we bring pain or happiness?
Who becomes the appointer?
  What should we focus on? Create?
  How much can we hold on our plate?

We strive for goals set from beyond?
Our DNA is encoded for an earthly destiny?
Who waves the magic wand?
Free will? Any input from me?
  Galactic Federations in charge?
  They shrink options or enlarge?

We are each other's magnitude and bond?
What is the purpose of this current embodiment?
Planetarary stewardship? Rather respond
to personal issues? A cosmic experiment?
  Does a veil of forgetfuless protect us?
  Who is empowered to select us?

Poems Previously Published:

Between our birth and our death we may touch understanding, as a moth brushes a window with its wing. Christopher Fry

Poetry Box: Thinking About Thoreau

Portland PEN:
>Dandelion Issue
>A Dandelion Miracle
>Slaughtering Dandelions
>A Dandelion Day
>Pauses of Sun
>In Defense of Dandelions
>Showering in Quarantine
>April Fools Day
>Aftermath
>The Lawn Lecture
>Dazzled By Dandelions
>In Chrysalis Mode
>Gently Falls the Rain
>Summer Before College

Other Poetry Books by Linda Varsell Smith

Cinqueries: A Cluster of Cinquos and Lanternes
Fibs and Other Truths
Black Stars on a White Sky
Poems That Count
Poems That Count Too
* Winging-It: New and Selected Poems
*Red Cape Capers: Playful Backyard Meditations
*Star Stuff: A Soul-Splinter Experiences the Cosmos
*Light-Headed: A Soul-Splinter Experiences Light
* Sparks: A Soul-Splinter Experiences Earth
* Into the Clouds: Seeking Silver Linings
*Mirabilia: Manifesting Marvels, Miracles and Mysteries
*Spiral Hands: Signs of Healing
*Lacunae: Mind the Gap
*Wayfinding: Navigating the Unknown
* Wordy-Smith: Dancing the Line
* Hugger-Muggery:Ways to Hugs and Mugs
* The Ground Crew: Beings with Earthly Experiences
* Waves: Ebbs and Flows
* Grounded With Gaia: Bonded with Earth
* Changes in Climate: Cleaning the Atmosphere

> * Available at www.Lulu.com/spotlight/rainbowcom

Chapbooks

Being Cosmic, Light-Headed, Intra-space Chronicles,
Red Cape Capers

On-Line Web-site Books:

Free-access @ RainbowComunications.org
Syllables of Velvet, Word-Playful, Poetluck

Anthologies: Poets Ponder Photographs, Poetic License,
Poetic License 2015, The Second Genesis, Jubilee, The
Eloquent Umbrella

Twelve novels in the Rainbow Chronicles Series